PERGAMON INSTITUTE OF ENGLISH (OXFORD)

Language Teaching Methodology Series

TESTING COMMUNICATIVE PERFORMANCE

Other titles in the series

TESTING COMMUNICATIVE PERFORMANCE

An Interim Study

BRENDAN J CARROLL

PERGAMON PRESS

Oxford · New York · Toronto · Sydney · Paris · Frankfurt

UK	Pergamon Press Ltd, Headington Hill Hall, Oxford OX3 0BW, England
USA	Pergamon Press Inc, Maxwell House, Fairview Park, Elmsford, New York 10523, USA
CANADA	Pergamon of Canada, Suite 104, 150 Consumers Road, Willowdale, Ontario M2J 1P9, Canada
AUSTRALIA	Pergamon Press (Aust) Pty Ltd, PO Box 544, Potts Point, NSW 2011, Australia
FRANCE	Pergamon Press SARL, 24 rue des Ecoles, 75240 Paris, Cedex 05, France
FEDERAL REPUBLIC OF GERMANY	Pergamon Press GmbH, 6242 Kronberg-Taunus, Pferdstrasse 1, Federal Republic of Germany

Copyright © 1980 Pergamon Press Ltd.

First edition 1980

British Library Cataloguing in Publication Data

Carroll, Brendan Joseph
Testing communicative performance. –
(Pergamon Institute of English (Oxford).
Language teaching methodology series.)
1. English language – Study and teaching –
Foreign students 2. English language –
Examinations 3. Grading and marking
(Students)
I. Title
428′.2′4076   PE1128.A2   79–42936

ISBN 0–08–024555–2 hardcover
ISBN 0–08–024554–4 flexicover

Printed in Great Britain by
A. Wheaton & Co. Ltd., Exeter

Contents

Foreword

During the past decade considerable changes have taken place in the field of language teaching – both in English as a Foreign or Second Language and in the teaching of foreign languages in general. In particular, it has been increasingly acknowledged that language is essentially a tool for communication and whereas grammatical patterns play a crucial role in communication, the prime need of most learners is not for a theoretical or analytical knowledge of the target language, but for an ability to understand and be understood in that language within the context and constraints of peculiar language-using circumstances.

In writing this book, I have set out to summarize the influence that this newly developed attitude has exerted on the essential concomitant of language learning – language testing. I have aimed to inform those concerned with language teaching about current thinking and practice, and to outline some of the outstanding problems, conscious that in doing so I run the risk on the one hand of being either too cryptic – in the interests of brevity – or on the other hand of being too detailed – in the interests of completeness. I hope that the note I have struck will not err too much on either side and that my readers will find some assistance in comprehending what has happened up to now, together with some pointers for the future. For it cannot be over-emphasized that we are now in a state of rapid change, and can certainly not yet claim to have mastered the challenge posed in my title – *Testing communicative performance.*

The ideas expressed in this book have been developed and modified in the light of experience gained on a number of projects in which I have been involved during the 1970's. It may be of interest to present a brief description of those projects.

1

Trial assessments were carried out in the British Council's English Language Teaching Institute in London, which runs short language courses, providing opportunities for pilot test projects; some of the results of these trials concerning cloze tests, indices of aptitude and the assessment of structured group discussions have proved to be of real importance. A more extensive project was the monitoring of a group of Venezuelan students, who did a year's preliminary course in English and Science before undertaking full-time tertiary studies in technical subjects: the major research result was to throw doubt, based on a series of principle component analyses, on the value of the typical test battery as an indication of communicative competence, since, although correlations with external competence assessments were statistically significant, the indications were that much of the common variance was not being explored by the proficiency tests used. In two sizeable projects in the Middle East over a period of four years, language tests have been developed for students of several major disciplines. Another project, in an ESL context, was carried out in an East African university, where students in a number of faculties were assessed as to their study-skills competence to determine if remedial programmes were necessary. A broad field for test development is provided in the British Council's English teaching operations in countries such as Indonesia, Greece, Germany, Italy and Portugal: because of the diversity of circumstances in which these courses are run, the full processes of pre-specification have not as yet been carried out, but initial proficiency tests have already been tried.

Further projects, of varying types, are: a new language examination for the Royal Society of Arts; certain modern language projects in Britain; a study of communication needs in a military headquarters; an evaluation of the progress of school students in a Gulf state; an evaluation of the effects of the use of media in a series of ODA – BBC – British Council language programmes. The largest, and probably most influential project has been the development of an English Language Testing Service for students wishing to undertake a variety of types of education or training in British institutions. This service, now pre-tested and being implemented, has taken a considerable time to develop because of its complex nature. In the event, what has emerged is a two-tier, flexible testing system, measuring the specified language skills of the major disciplinary fields in which training is required by overseas students. The above provides experience with some 7,000 testees in about twelve different testing situations in various parts of the world over a period of five years. During this time, many different approaches and analyses have been made and a number of test strategies have been examined.

It is from this experience that I have presented the procedures described in this book, while stressing that a considerable amount of work still remains to be done before it can be said that the main problems of testing communicative performance have been solved. My special thanks are due to the guidance and assistance of my colleagues: John Munby, Shelagh Rixon, Ian Seaton, Roger Hawkey, Mel Hughes, David Herbert, Elizabeth Smyth and Peter Brown. The judgements and attitudes stated and implied are my own, and though I am heavily indebted to my colleagues, past and present (as I have tried to make clear within the text), the responsibility for any deficiencies is mine alone. My thanks are also due to members of my family – Patricia, Moira, Fiona and Imelda for their help with typing and indexing.

Brendan J Carroll
Newbury
January 1980

1. The assessment of communicative performance

The purpose of this book is to outline principles and techniques for specifying the communicative needs of a language learner and for assessing his language performance in terms of those needs. A central place is given to the use of such assessments for making decisions about the placement and progress of learners on language programmes; the main thesis can thus be expressed in terms of the 'curriculum triangle':

Figure 1: The curriculum triangle

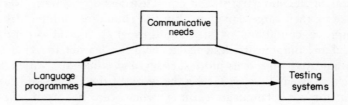

This diagram illustrates the key role played by the specification of *communicative needs* in the development of language curricula, and the derivation of the design of both language programmes and testing systems from this specification. We cannot, however, draw from the specification of needs any direct imperatives about the pedagogy of the programmes or the nature of the testing instruments; such factors will depend on the resources and time available and on the inherent demands of teaching and testing. Therefore, the initial specification should not be seen as a straitjacket clamped on to the curriculum but as a comprehensive and detailed compendium giving unity and purpose to it. The diagram thus illustrates the interactive relationship between the language programme and the testing system, and their mutual derivation from an analysis of the learner's communicative needs.

Traditionally, programmes do not generally exemplify this tripartite congruence of needs, programmes and tests. Typically, needs are often vaguely specified in terms equally applicable to a wide range of learners, and thus specific to none of them; language programmes are devoted to the acquisition of lexical and syntactic items with little systematic consideration of the communicative aims of the individual learner; and tests or examinations are only loosely or fortuitously related either to the learner's needs or to the content of his learning programme. Unfortunately, in many language courses the end examination not only provides the learning motivation but dominates the content and pedagogy of the courses, thus inverting the priorities illustrated in our diagram.

In practice, of course, a good deal of work can be done by a skilful teacher and a diligent student to compensate for the deficiencies of an illogical curriculum pattern, and many learners do ultimately succeed in learning their target language. But this should not inhibit attempts to improve conditions of learning through a logical ordering of curriculum components designed to help the learner to achieve his communicative objectives more speedily and efficiently. An example of such a systematic approach is the work of the Council of Europe project for adult language learning, where care has been taken to specify the purposes for which European Community members are likely to communicate with each other, and language courses and tests are being developed from them. Some of the projects described above are also producing results, so that the ideas already outlined are not merely untried theory.

Communication and language

The development of tests for assessing communicative performance has been greatly influenced by current ideas about the role of language in communication and, in particular, by the implications of those ideas for the teaching and testing of languages for specific purposes (LSP).

Approaches to problems of language testing are strongly influenced by the place accorded to *usage* and *use* in inter-personal communication. This dichotomy, lucidly expounded by Widdowson (1978), echoes the long-discussed distinctions between *langue* and *parole* and between competence and performance. Concentration on *usage* is concerned primarily with formal language patterns, whereas *use* is concerned with communicative function, with how the language is used. Pedagogies emphasizing usage build on the selection and sequencing of learning units expressed in formal linguistic terms (the definite article, plurals, the conditional tense), even if they do not actually employ these labels, and give a good deal of importance to the formal correctness of the learner's usage. Programmes emphasizing use, however, base their pedagogies on effective communication, assuming that realistic communication will provide the learner with meaningful practice, so that he will conform gradually to the norms of usage, the emphasis being on appropriacy rather than formal linguistic correctness. The hope is, on the one hand, that continued practice in usage will ultimately produce effective use and, on the other, that continual use will produce appropriate usage.

It is easy to see how either of these approaches could go badly wrong; the *usage* emphasis could result in a mastery of sentence patterns coupled with an inability to use them in day-to-day communication; the *use* emphasis could lead to fluency in a pidgin language embarrassing to the user and unintelligible to the listener. Of course, no teacher would wish to induce either of these extremes: it is a question of emphasis and priorities. For the present writer there is little doubt where the priorities lie. The *use* of a language is the *objective*, and the mastery of the formal patterns, or *usage*, of that language is a *means* to achieve this objective. The ultimate criterion of language mastery is therefore the learner's effectiveness in communication for the settings he finds himself in.

The distinction between *usage* and *use* is of great importance for teaching and testing. It implies that a test cannot be based on a selection of items chosen on linguistic grounds alone, and that to devise an effective test, it is necessary to specify how a testee requires to use the language. The criterion for success lies not in formal correctness but in communicative effectiveness. One should not, however, oversimplify the complex relationship between usage and use. Whilst it is clear that a fully competent native user of a language will have little trouble in selecting those language forms which will best serve his functional requirements, it is not so evident that this will apply also to a non-native learner in the early stages of language acquisition. To extend the Hymes (1974) assertion that 'there are rules of use without which the rules of grammar would be useless', we might add 'there are rules of grammar without which the rules of use would be inoperable'. .

Changing the emphasis from usage to use means also changing ideas concerning the specificity of tests. From the *usage* point of view, a language can be seen as a unified entity with fixed grammatical patterns and a core of commonly-used lexical items. Equipped with a mastery of these language patterns, it is hoped the user will learn to cope with the situations he finds himself in. Therefore a single test of the learner's language proficiency based on formal usage should prove an adequate indication of his ability to cope with real situations. But from the point of view of the role of language in communication, such a view is greatly oversimplified. Different patterns of communication will entail different configurations of language skill mastery, and therefore a different course or test content. From the *use* point of view, language loses its appearance of unity and must be taught and tested according to the specific needs of the learner.

Hitherto, few courses have been designed with the specific purposes of particular learners in mind. Courses in 'Intermediate English' or 'Advanced French' are conducted indiscriminately for doctors, waiters, students and tourists. Even courses purporting to teach, say, 'English for Doctors' may turn out to be language-based programmes founded, not on carefully-conducted job analyses, but on educated guesses and casual observation of the communicative activities of doctors, recognizing that they have special needs but lacking the techniques needed to specify those needs in detail. There are also many 'general' courses for those who have no specific objectives or for groups of learners with heterogeneous needs. But when a language need is specific and time is short, there is surely no efficient alternative to devising, or drawing on, specially-prepared courses designed to meet such specified needs.

The adoption of the criteria of communicative use presents many difficulties to the tester, and it is not claimed that as yet they have been overcome. It would, no doubt, be much more comfortable to stay with the concept of general proficiency tests, based on usage, because the alternative concept of diversified testing bristles with difficulties. But the writer believes that such diversified tests are the only logical answer to the communicative problem, and we shall explore the principles and practice of such tests.

Issues in communicative testing

We deal now with certain issues particularly related to the devising of instruments for measuring communicative behaviour.

The first problem is to discover how to carry out a rigorous measurement of language-based performance and yet keep intact the essential features of communicative behaviour. One accepted solution has been to pick out particular language features, especially those likely to cause difficulties, present them one after the other in a test and assess the testee's general proficiency from the number to which he gives a 'correct' response. The danger is that in building up easily-devised and objectively-scored tests of strings of linguistic items we may miss the essence of the measurement of communicative performance. Detaching test items from their communicative context is to risk finding little about the learner's behaviour which is not trivial; and merely multiplying the number of trivia is not going to solve the measurement problem.

It might be argued that one answer to the isolated or discrete approach to item writing is the *cloze test*. But this is still essentially usage-based.

The task does not represent genuine interactive communication and is therefore only an indirect index of potential efficiency in coping with day-to-day communicative tasks.

Another focus of discussion has been the distinction between *norm-referenced* and *criterion-referenced* tests, ie between comparing the performance of an individual with that of other individuals in a sample of comparable persons, as against comparing his performance with pre-determined behavioural criteria. These two approaches are not mutually exclusive and both can contribute to the solution of testing problems in that the primary point of reference in the *design* of tests, the *analysis* of test items and the *interpretation* of test performance is the specified, communicative, behavioural criterion. The use of norm-based statistics (refer to page 100 ff. below) can be of help in certain aspects of item analysis and the interpretation of test performance. Insights into communicative behaviour are not yet sufficient for us to abandon statistical, inferential techniques, though we are no longer so heavily dependent on such techniques. Emphasis on the pre-specification of communicative tasks lends itself to criterion-referenced techniques, but it is far too early to consider dispensing with the elaborate and well-worked-out procedures of norm-based statistics.

In a recently-published document, a new test, described as being 'criterion-referenced', includes in the performance rating sheet the three categories of 'vocabulary', 'grammar' and 'pronunciation'. But such categories are essentially those of language-based usage: they refer not to the final criteria of communicative performance but to contributory and subordinate 'enabling' skills related to, but not identical with, communicative skills. In this book the term 'criterion-referenced' will refer to criteria of specified communicative behaviour, not to contributory linguistic skills. In the performance criteria described in Appendix III, priority is given to descriptions of actual communicative behaviour such as, *Can handle interjections, responds to tones, etc.* Only in so far as they clarify the level of performance of such behaviour do we bring in specifically linguistic or usage features such as *Can interpret accurately lexical and grammatical usage and the significance of variations in tone and stress patterns.* In other words, our criteria are communicative behavioural features which subsume the liguistically-based skills used for performing the task.

The reason for this priority is associated with the fact that any one communicative activity or function can be realized in a number of language patterns. If we wish to test the ability to 'suggest', for example, we may elicit a number of utterances:

> *I suggest that* . . . . .
> *What about* . . . . *-ing*
> *If I were you I'd* . . . .

or just the Nominal Group . . . . *The* **football** *match:*

or

> *Nonsense*
> *Mmm* . . . . .
> *Hm* . . *Hm* . .

or even a pregnant silence.

Any of these responses may allow the testee to achieve his communicative purpose but it is virtually impossible to predict which one will be used. The adequacy of his response will depend both on the extent of his linguistic resources and on his skill in deploying them; on whether he uses a limited stock confidently and effectively or flounders and misuses a considerable and sophisticated usage stock. The important point is that it is the *use* of the language and not just the possession of the tools of *usage* that ultimately decides the user's effectiveness in handling communicative situations. Anyone who has spent many years learning Latin and remained utterly unable to communicate in it will readily appreciate this particular point. It is not always (to switch our example) the player with the shiniest golf clubs who wins the game.

The issue of *authenticity* must always be an important aspect of any discussion on language testing. A full application of the principle of authenticity would mean that all the tasks undertaken should be real-life, interactive communicative operations and not the typical routine examination responses to the tester's 'stimuli', or part of a stimulus-response relationship; that the language of the test should be day-to-day discourse, not edited or doctored in the interests of simplification but presented with all its expected irregularities; that the contexts of the interchanges are realistic, with the ordinary interruptions, background noises and irrelevancies found in the air-port or lecture-room; and that the rating of a performance, based on its effectiveness and adequacy as a communicative response, will rely on non-verbal as well as verbal criteria.

It is easy to see how different from these are many of the language tests of today. What could be less authentic in the task it sets the testee, the language stimulus it provides, or the assessment of the value of his response than a multiple-choice item of language structure such as:

	(a) *doesn't he?*
He eats meat, ...	(b) *won't I?*
	(c) *can't you?*

Even those test tasks which require the use of real, live language usually do so in a very artificial setting – *Describe in 75–100 words how a bicycle works* – and unreal assignments such as this, which few people would undertake in ordinary life. Or consider the tasks lying midway between the closed multiple-choice item and the open-ended writing example just given, such as a cloze test, in which one is asked to replace every fifth word. It is claimed that this is a test of basic linguistic processing mechanisms, of the grammar of prediction, but is it a credible communicative task? It seems, as Morrow (1979) maintains, that conventional tests ignore certain features of genuine language use, which are that language is interactive, unpredictable, purposive, authentic, contextualized, based in performance and assessed in terms of behavioural outcomes. Indeed, it could be claimed that at present we are not testing genuine communicative performance at all, but artificial, language-like behaviour.

The question is, 'In order to measure communication, do we *have* to trivialize it first?' If the answer is yes, then we will have to be satisfied with testing pseudo-communication; if no, then we must search for more satisfactory measuring techniques.

Authenticity in itself cannot provide the total answer to the testing problem, nor can tests be constructed simply by putting together a random selection of tasks, however authentic. Test tasks must be drawn from a range of inter-related systems, from consciously systematized functions, skills and linguistic categories, brought together in the performance of an authentic communicative operation; performances whose value is judged by reference to the satisfactory resolution of patterns of communication, function, skill and language in an effective system of language measurement.

Phases in test construction

The three phases in the construction of a testing system are as shown in Figure 2.

Figure 2: Test construction phases

Phase 1: *Design*	(1) description of participant(s); (2) analysis of communicative needs; (3) specification of test content.
Phase 2: *Development*	(4) realization of tests; (5) trial application; (6) validation and test analysis.
Phase 3: *Operation*	(7) full-scale application; (8) operational use; (9) revision of test system.

These phases are discussed in Chapters 2, 3 and 4 (below).

Before describing the processes of test construction, we may stipulate the characteristics we would wish a test to possess. They may be summarized as:

$$\left.\begin{array}{l} \text{Relevance} \\ \text{Acceptability} \\ \text{Comparability} \\ \text{Economy} \end{array}\right\} - \text{RACE}$$

A good test will show an optimum balance of these four characteristics.

Relevance: *How relevant is the behaviour being tested to the meeting of communicative needs?*

Certain types of test behaviour are more directly relevant than others to the behaviour required in the performance of communicative tasks. Because of the constraints of testing, it is advisable to go straight for the criterion communicative behaviour, except in diagnostic testing, which is concerned with the mechanisms underlying performance. Relevance may be established in a number of ways. There are two overriding criteria: first, the extent to which the test reflects the specifications identified in an analysis of communicative needs: second, the extent to which the test information is able to guide decisions about the testee.

The needs analysis technique cited here as the basis of test content specification is that of J L Munby, who describes his techniques fully in *Communicative syllabus design*, Cambridge University Press, 1978. The test design procedures given below owe much to this comprehensive and systematic approach, and the descriptions of test development will be the more readily appreciated by reference to it, since it describes in detail the procedures for identifying the communicative needs of a learner or group of learners which, presented as a needs profile, facilitate specification of the content of a syllabus or test in terms of language skills and functions, which may in turn be realized in appropriate language forms. The primary criterion for relevance is the extent to which the tests reflect the needs specified in the analysis.

As our basic evaluation paradigm is the decision-facilitation model, a major criterion lies in the proven value of the test information to the makers of decisions about the testees. We outline the main decision areas in our description of the operation of a test system. We thus check the operational value of the initial analysis against the final decision-making criterion. During test development, interim criteria to provide a first approximation of standards may also be employed.

Acceptability: *Will the users of the test accept its content and format?*

The introduction of formal testing immediately puts all programme users under a strain. But unless the testees cooperate fully and the administering staff ensure that the test procedures are followed in the spirit and to the letter, the data provided are much reduced in value. The climate of opinion about testing methods may be such that any violent switches from conventional procedures could unduly disturb the participants.

In testing projects in which the author has participated, considerations of acceptability have been of some importance and have occasionally caused considerable modification of the advice proffered, so that tests have sometimes been less use-based than would otherwise have been desirable. In an international context, too, in a whole range of cultural contexts, care is needed to avoid topics potentially offensive to religious or social susceptibilities, which might destroy all cooperation.

Comparability: *Can the test scores obtained at different times and from different groups be compared?*

The first basis of comparison is between learner and target performance. Then, within the criteria based on the initial specification and ultimate decision-making, a stable standard of measurement has to be provided, so that the performance of one person or group can be compared with that of others, or the performance of a person on one occasion can be compared with his performance on another. Such comparisons are often necessary when making decisions about placement or progress. We may wish to compare an individual's levels of performance at different stages of his programme or, in an experimental project, to compare the rates of improvement between groups subjected to various conditions of learning.

Without stable measuring instruments, it will not be possible to establish whether differences in scores reflect genuine differences in standards or are a product of the unreliability of the test instrument. In ESP[1], widespread comparisons are often not possible (and, indeed, there is little logic in comparing essentially disparate programmes) but most course organizers welcome the chance of some objective basis upon which to make comparisons between various learning groups.

Economy: *Do the tests provide as much information as is required with the minimum expenditure of time, effort and resources?*

As time and resources invested in testing usually have to be subtracted from the activities of the programme as a whole, any investment in formal testing should ensure the maximum essential information. This implies that in a given situation we must first query whether formal testing is in fact necessary, and the answer must frequently be that it is not. The next query is how little testing can be done to provide sufficient data for the making of decisions; the answer again is frequently that we can obtain the data with very little testing.

Careful questioning of this kind may ensure that, when tests are really needed, they will be made and used effectively. One way in which economy can be effected is to use rapid subjective assessments on carefully-devised rating criteria and to scale those subjective assessments upon objectively-devised test scores.

We shall return to these four basic test characteristics in our descriptions of test development.

Note

[1] English for Specific Purposes.

2. The design of communicative tests

Principles of design

As described in Chapter 1, the design phase consists of:

- description of participant;
- analysis of his communicative needs;
- specification of test content.

The various processes required to make our specification of test content are shown in the figure below, which is a modification of that of Munby (*op cit* p 33 ff).

Figure 3: Communicative competence specification

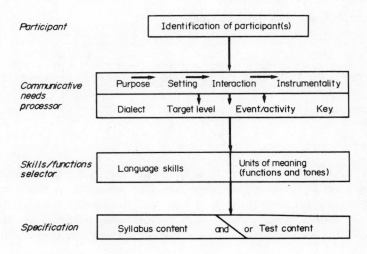

The parameters of this model are essentially functional. There is a general tendency for designers to get down to actual language realizations before the completion of the functional specification. There is a similar tendency to bring in premature pedagogical or logistical considerations whilst still specifying needs. Indeed, the above model has been criticized because it ignores such pedagogical and logistical constraints. But the fact is that communicative needs exist independently of their linguistic realizations and regardless of whether or not they will form the basis of a learning programme. The demand for such a programme only becomes apparent when there is a gap between the level of performance of the participant and the requirements revealed by the needs analysis.

Appendices I and II give fully worked-out communication needs profiles which illustrate, in different contexts, the initial stages in test (or programme) design.

In contrast to the complex model just described, we shall examine a comparatively crude one (which takes much less specific account of the special needs of an individual or of the communicative features subsumed above), comprising a simple skill/level matrix (Figure 4).

Figure 4: Guide test design model

Skills / Levels	Production		Reception	
	Writing	Speaking	Reading	Listening
Phonology Vocabulary Grammar Context				

This is, I believe, too crude a basis for specifying the complex parameters and relationships of linguistic communication, but it may be adequate for testing usage in a general proficiency context, and certain general-purpose tests with performance norms have been derived from it. Being more crude than that shown in Figure 3 this model will also be a less precise guide to programme content and thus be less fruitful for effecting test-programme congruence.

The analytical procedure adopted will be illustrated by referring to two communication needs profiles. The first is a profile of the needs of a Nigerian student who wishes to take a Business Studies course in Britain (Appendix I)[1]. The second is a profile of the needs of young overseas visitors who wish to use English to meet the day-to-day demands of living for a time in Britain (Appendix II)[2]. The first profile is in the area of English for Academic or Educational Purposes (EAP), the second is rather less specific and could be named English for Social Survival. In the following sections we will describe the specification parameters given in Figure 3.

Communicative needs analysis (from the example in Appendix I)

Participant identification

We identify our participant by giving relevant information about his identity and language background, such as his age, sex, nationality and place of residence as well as target language (in this case, English), mother tongue and any other languages learnt. Although we may be studying the needs of one participant, it is likely that he will act as a prototype for a number of learners with similar aspirations.

Purpose

The occupational or educational purposes for which the participant will need to use the target language are now specified. Here, the purpose is educational in the specific discipline of Business Studies, within which are the study areas of Economics, Law and Accountancy.

Setting

The parameter of setting embraces both physical setting (country, place, institution and type of work) and psycho-social setting (cultural type, sophistication, pace).

Interaction

The persons with whom the participant will deal in his education and the inter-relationships involved are stated. The social relationships will be of considerable importance when we come to the linguistic features involved in expressing or interpreting tones.

Instrumentality

The input in terms of *medium* (spoken, written etc), *mode* (dialogue, written to be spoken, etc) and *channel* (face-to-face, telephone, print, etc) are specified.

The four parameters above are independent variables referred to in specifying the following four dependent variables:

Dialect

From the many varieties of the language concerned we select those which it is appropriate for our participant to produce or understand. For our sample participant it will be appropriate to produce a Standard West African English with a Northern Nigerian accent and to understand British Standard English with RP (Received Pronunciation) or near RP accent plus the main accents of Southern England, Wales and Scotland.

Target level

The target level for the participant's command of English is specified in terms of the dimensions of size, complexity, range, delicacy, speed and flexibility. Tolerance conditions for error, style, reference, repetition and hesitation are also established. For the purpose of devising tests, we will modify the target level parameter given in Munby (*op cit*), but here present it in its original terms as a guide to programme design. It may be noted that the EAP student will normally be expected to have a higher level of receptive skill mastery than of production skill, thus emphasizing his role as a collector rather than dispenser of information.

Events/activities

The event parameter covers the main focuses of the education the participant is expected to undergo. In this instance, he must attend lectures, write reports, take part in seminars and so on. He will also have to make visits to industrial and commercial locations, dealing with staff on a non-academic basis. In addition, he will have to live in an English-using environment, for which purpose our specification in Appendix II should be relevant. The macro-category of 'event' is divided into smaller-scale constituents, named 'activities', which will later permit of more direct skill and function realizations. Thus the event, 'Attending lectures', may be broken down into the constituent activities, *Listening for overall comprehension, Taking notes to be reconstituted* and *Asking questions for clarification of lecture content*, such activities being, at a later stage, broken down in terms of language skills and/or units of meaning.

Communicative key

The final variable is that of key, which allows us to specify how the activities are carried out. A study of the earlier variables will indicate how to specify the likely attitudes, or keys, that the participant will be required to produce or understand for each event. Guidance as to key will be found in an attitudinal tone index (Munby, p 168 ff) in which a number of *continua* eg 'formal – informal' with the more likely exponents of each continuum presented as co-hyponyms such as, *ceremonious/correct/detached* or *casual/familiar/intimate*. The parameter of key is of great potential importance because it is in interpreting interpersonal attitudes that non-native speakers often face their greatest problems and that language programmes are at their most deficient.

Selection of language skills

Having assembled the data for a communicative needs profile, we are now in a position to select the specific language skills and units of meaning needed to carry out the activities specified. We will deal with the language skills in the present section and with units of meaning in the next.

The taxonomy of language skills, containing some 260 micro-skills in 54 skill categories, is perhaps the most immediately useful aspect of our needs specification model. Although not so divided in the original taxonomy, the language skills can be seen to fall into several broad fields, as follows:

- *oral and aural skills*, especially stress and intonation;
- *graphic skills*, especially spelling and punctuation;
- *language patterns* within the sentence, particularly those conveying information and conceptual meaning through lexical and structural devices;
- *discourse features*, such as indicators for handling a topic and indicating the structure of a discourse; such features make a text what it is rather than a string of separate sentences;
- *reference study and situation-handling skills* for handling or relaying information.

The language skill taxonomy in Appendix 1 selects those skills needed for a Business Studies course. It can easily be seen how directly the language skills item bank can lead to the devising of a language programme likely to meet specified needs.

Units of meaning

The current emphasis on socio-linguistic features of communication is seen in the central place we afford to psycho-social setting and social relationships, which inform the communicative key. The activities specified are now ready to be processed into communicative functions which, accompanied by their appropriate attitudinal tone markers, are called 'units of meaning'. We illustrate this rather complex definition by drawing on one of the specified events in Appendix 1 – *Student attending lectures in his area of study* – and on one of the constituent activities – *Asking for clarification*. The productive micro-function needed is 'query' and, in the particular setting specified, this function will be carried out courteously and rather formally. We may illustrate this combination of function and attitudinal tone – the unit of meaning – in the following summary:

Event: Student attending lectures.
Activity: Asking for clarification.
Function: (productive) Query.
Tones: Courteous, formal.
Unit of meaning: Query [+ courteous], [+ formal].
Realization: 'Excuse me, I wonder if you could explain again the relationship between (x) and (y). I'm not quite sure exactly how they connect.' In circumstances when authenticity is important, we shall select from authentic utterances rather than produce such synthetic texts as the above.

On the receptive side, the student making the query will have to recognize, from the verbal clues given by the lecturer, to what extent the explanation is rational, authoritative etc. Again, we have a function (explain) marked for attitude [+ rational], [+ authoritative] constituting a unit of meaning. Perception of merely the surface structure of the reply might be misleading if, as may sometimes happen, the lecturer were to reply sarcastically or in a jocular fashion.

Specification of test content

By making the analysis just described, we have been able to produce a profile of communicative needs as a guide for the selection of language skills and/or units of meaning which is then ready for realization in actual language for both programmes and tests. It is at this stage that the item writers and test constructors can be given clear guidance about the kind of test they are expected to devise. (If the test is of any size, and if we have several test constructors, such a detailed guide is necessary to ensure the harmonization of all the components of the test system.)

The realization of design specifications in actual tests is an exciting job if done on a team basis, and one requiring the reconciliation of scientific criteria and creative talent.

To reduce the complexities of the task of the test devisers, we have modified the above specification procedures along the lines shown in Figure 5. In this table, we are given procedures for item construction which draw on information collected in ten information banks.

Figure 5: Parameters and procedures for test design

	Information banks	Procedural guide
1	Participant identification	Broadly describe typical participant.
2	Purpose for language use	Describe main uses of English and classify under ESP headings: academic, occupational or social survival.
3	Events/activities	Choose the major events to be met with, and select several activities for each.
4	Instrumentality	Select media — listening, speaking, reading or writing, or multiple-mode combinations. Channels: face-to-face, tape, print, film, etc.
5	Socio-cultural	Specify social relationships, dialect and socio-cultural factors.
6	Performance levels	Using nine-point scale, give target levels of performance for each medium and multiple-mode.
7	Topic areas	Identify semantic areas for each specified event.
8	Language skills	Choose the skills necessary for carrying out the different activities at given target levels.
9	Language function/ tones units	Indicate functions needed, and appropriate attitudinal tones, for those activities involving sizeable person-to-person interactions.
10	Test format	Choose types of item for each activity — closed-ended, open-ended or restricted response (note RACE and authenticity).

When the team approach to test development is used, the contents of the information banks are devised and discussed by all team members. Thereafter, the team is divided into sub-groups to deal with test areas assigned to them. In EAP test development, it is necessary to have inter-disciplinary sub-groups with experienced teachers of the target language working side-by-side with people qualified in the particular discipline for which tests are being devised, eg Engineering, Social Sciences or Medicine. The characteristics of *relevance, acceptability, comparability* and *economy* (RACE) are to be borne constantly in mind.

Detailed test item construction procedures

We will now exemplify the main test construction procedures in accordance with the ten information banks shown in Figure 5, and in accordance with the specifications given in Appendices I and II. Appropriate Appendix references are given in each section below.

Participant identification

(Ref: Appendix I, O, page 106)

Our first participant is the young Nigerian wishing to have training in Business Studies.

Our second specification is a broader one, bringing in a range of participants with the common communicative need of using 'in-Britain English'. It is possible that ESP purists might see this second category as being too broad to be subsumed under a single needs profile but, in practice, we have found this procedure to be both feasible and stimulating.

Purpose for language use

(Ref: Appendix I, 1, page 107)

The first specification comes under the classification, English for

Academic Purposes, the second may be classified as English for Social Survival.

Events/activities

(Refs: Appendices 1, 7, page 112, II Banks 4 + 5, page 124)

The academic events for our first participant consist of lectures, seminars, reference studies, report writing, general reference and course-related visits. The second participant will encounter no less than eleven major events, including visiting places of interest, shopping and using services, getting medical attention, studying for interest and dealing with officials. These events sub-divide into activities of which some events have as many as ten.

Instrumentality

(Refs: Appendices, I, 4, page 109, II, Bank 2, page 123)

In more recent test development we have had to question the communicative credibility of the traditional classification of listening, speaking, reading and writing. For example, if communication is essentially interactive, in what authentic communicative context can we test pure listening? The contribution to the communicative activity by a participant who hears something meaningful is to respond in speech, in writing or by carrying out some action which indicates an appropriate response in the communicative chain. We illustrate our thesis by reference to Figure 6, in which we place the traditional four main macro-activities of listening, speaking, reading and writing in their communicative context, bearing in mind the essentially interactive nature of language.

Communicative interaction is shown in one direction as *conversation* (the oral skills of listening and speaking) and, in the other direction, as *correspondence* (the graphic skills of reading and writing). In various situations, we may use such combinations as hearing, talking, studying and composing to make more precise the broad, and rather impersonal terms generally used. The diagram illustrates the relationships between verbal and non-verbal modes, between immediate, putative and delayed responses, between reception and production and between oral and graphic discourse.

Figure 6: Media for communicative interaction

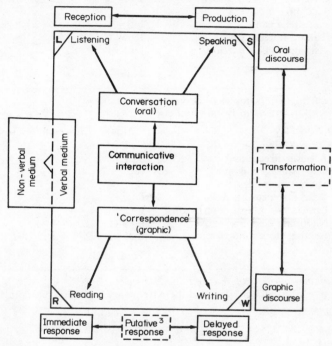

The various ways in which combinations of modes occur in daily life are worked out using the two specifications and summarized in Figure 7 (A), (B) and (C).

In *Academic English*, to judge from the subjective ratings made, four permutations represent nearly 90% of the modes, namely:

Reading (R)	(Studying)	31 (%)
Reading and *writing* (W)	(Note-making/reference)	23
Listening (L) and *speaking* (S)	(Conversing)	22
Listening (L) *and writing* (W)	(Lectures/notes)	11

Figure 7: Estimates of mode combinations

(A) *Business Studies* (samples from Academic English)
   Event 7.2 Student participating in seminars and tutorials

Activities	Modes	Frequency[4]	Survival[5]
1. Discussing topics presented	L+S	2	3
2. Listening for overall comprehension	L	2	4
3. Taking notes	L+W	2	3
4. Asking for clarification	L+S+R	1	3
Total (20)		7	13

(B) *Social English* (samples of Social Survival English)
   Event 5.4 Travel in Britain and elsewhere

Activities	Modes	Frequency	Survival
1. State destination	S+L	3	4
2. Ask for directions	S+L	4	4
3. Understand road signs	R	2	2
4. Study time-tables	R	2	2
5. Read instructions, maps	R	3	2
6. Understand maps, descriptions	L+R	1	1
7. Negotiate customs	L+S+R	1	4
8. Arrange accommodation	L+S+R+W	2	4
Total (41)		18	23

(C) *Comparison of Academic and Social Modes* (%)
   (drawn from all activities and their frequency and survival indices)

Academic English			Social English		
Rank Order	Modes	%	Rank Order	Modes	%
1	R	31	1	L+S	49
2	R+W	23	2	R	21
3	L+S	22	3	R+W	12
4	L+W	11	4	L	4
5	L	8	5	L+S+R	4
6	L+R+S	5	6	W	3
			7	R+L	3
		100	8	S	2
			9	L+S+R+W	2
					100

In *Social English*, 90% of the index coverage is
   represented by:

Listening and *speaking*	(Conversing)	49	(%)
Reading	(Reading)	21	
Reading and *writing*	(Corresponding)	12	
Listening	(Listening in)	4	
Listening, speaking and *reading*	(Discussing/reference)	4	

For testing purposes, there is a high probability that the mode permutations: L+S (Conversation/discussion), R (Reading/studying) and R+W (Corresponding/notemaking), possibly adding in L+W (Note-taking), cover the bulk of a learner's communicative requirements. The isolated modes – writing, speaking and listening – seem to represent rather unrealistic tasks and testing them in isolation takes one a step away from reality.

It may be said that the mixed-mode test is 'impure' and that we will not know precisely which mode we are testing. This is perfectly true and would be disconcerting if our orientation were towards language usage. But we are not primarily concerned with testing usage but with assessing a person's capability to cope with specified communicative tasks. In short, for test construction the separate modes of listening, speaking and writing, whilst possibly acceptable as discrete analytical categories, are unlikely to correspond to the realities of interactive behaviour; but mixed categories such as discussion, studying/researching and correspondence are likely to be more authentic focuses.

Socio-cultural factors

At this level, information from three areas will prove significant: namely, the relationship between the interlocuters (see *Setting* in Appendix I, 3, page 109), the varieties of language used (see *Dialect* in Appendix I, 5, page 110), and any special cultural features which may affect the units of meaning.

Performance levels

(Refs: Appendix I, 6, page 111, II, Bank 3, page 124)

It is a long-established convention that the results of tests and examinations be expressed in quantitative scores (27/40 or 38%), in rank orders (third out of twenty), or in some sort of grade or band (B on an A–E scale, or 3 on a 1–10 scale), a basic assumption about such scales being that B is a 'better' grade than C, that 34 is a 'better' score than 28, that being third is 'better' than being eighth. With grades, such as A–E or 1–10, it is often assumed that the intervals are equal, that C is better than D to the same extent that B is better than C. With scores or percentages, however, this assumption is not usually made; 31 is not necessarily as much better than 30 as 12 is better than 11. A final assumption is that, in any sizeable group of testees, scores or grades will cluster around a central point (expressed as a mean) and will have a distribution (expressed as a standard deviation) about that central point. Obtained scores will be of high frequency near the mean, but will fall in frequency the more the score diverges from that mean. Expressed as a histogram or graph, this distribution will give us the familiar bell-shaped curve of the 'normal distribution'. From time to time, and variously for different purposes, we will draw on the above assumptions when discussing test scores or standards.

Our working thesis is that test performances can be allocated to a nine-point language band scale, either directly by rating a particular performance as being that specified for, say, Band 4, or, indirectly, by converting raw test scores into a standard 'L' (language) score which may be converted to the 1–9 Band system by dividing by ten. For example, a raw score of 43/50 would be read off a transformation table as a standard 'L' score of, say, 73 which is comparable to a Band score of 7.3, that is, near the bottom of the seventh Band. We describe the mechanics of score transformation and interpretation in the next chapter, but introduce the topic here to put in context the performance criteria needed to construct test performance scales.

Performance criteria

Our performance scales (exemplified in Appendix III) are derived from ten performance criteria which we describe below:

1. *Size*, the physical extent of the text (oral or graphic) being produced or comprehended.
2. *Complexity*, the extent to which the focuses of a text multiply in regard to topics, styles of presentation and semantic fields.
3. *Range*, the variety of skills, functions and tones presented in a text.
4. *Speed*, the speed at which a task is performed.
5. *Flexibility*, the ability to adapt to novelty and switches in the features of a task presented.
6. *Accuracy*, the extent to which the candidate has mastered correct, formal usage, and the correctness of the information he draws from or presents in a text.
7. *Appropriacy*, the degree to which the style of task performance corresponds to the legitimate expectations of other users.
8. *Independence*, the degree of independence of reference sources and questioning of his interlocuters.
9. *Repetition*, the extent to which a user needs to re-read a text, or ask for repeats of an utterance.
10. *Hesitation*, the degree of delay in starting a task and the occurrence of hesitation in performing it.

It is through these performance criteria that we realize the central feature of our test system, namely, *to confront the testee with a communicative task*. The criteria may relate either to the task or to the testee's performance. For example, he may be presented with a long text which, other things being equal, should be a more difficult task to cope with than a short text. Equally, he may be expected to produce a long utterance which, again other things being equal, should be a more difficult task to handle than a short utterance. Similarly, it is more difficult to perform with a high degree of accuracy or appropriacy, and a higher rating will be given for such performances. In applying tests we may either present a number of tasks of varying difficulty, producing performances at corresponding levels, or present a single task and rate the testees according to the level at which they perform it.

The construction of performance scales (samples of which are shown in Appendix III) and the allocating of tasks and testee performance to those scales is a subjective matter, but we will show later how the disadvantages and advantages of subjectivity can be balanced. At the initial stages in test development, we will have to establish rather crude, interim scales to guide us. We may well start with defining three levels of task difficulty. The first scale will represent the level of completely satisfactory performance for the job required (Target level); the second will specify the lowest level of performance which it is deemed appropriate to test at all (Basic level), and the third will be a level midway between these two poles (Intermediate level). For young school children in a non-English using area, for example, these three levels might equate to Bands 1, 2, and 3 on our nine-point scale. For post-graduate medical students in Britain, on the other hand, the appropriate three levels might be Bands 4, 6 and 8 on our scale (see Figure 9 below for examples of the nine-point scale descriptions).

Topic areas

(Refs: Appendix I, 7, page 112; II Bank 6, page 128)

The events and activities already specified will be important guides for selecting the topic areas of our tests. In the first specification, that for Business Studies, the topics will be derived from the subjects to be studied, namely, Economics, Law and Accountancy, etc. In the second specification, for the event, 'Obtaining medical attention', the topic areas will be illnesses, symptoms, parts of the body, medicines, etc. From these sources we could, if we wished, build up banks of lexical items for teaching or testing, always remembering to operate in meaningful contexts.

Language skills

(Refs: Appendix I, 9 page 115; II, Bank 9, page 132)

We have found the taxonomy of 54 language skills set out in Munby (1978, p 123 ff) to be one of the most fruitful sources of information for test construction. A general description of the taxonomy has already been given above on page 22. In Appendix I, section 9, a range of skills is specified for the Business Studies participant. In selecting skills it is wise to choose first those broader skills towards the end of the taxonomy, say, from skill 39 onwards, and only to deal specifically with lower order intra-sentential and segmental skills (eg lexical or phonetic phenomena) when it becomes necessary to probe the mastery of language mechanisms needed for the exercising of communicative skills. It is not easy to find authentic contexts for testing these lower order, sometimes called 'enabling', skills.

Language functions/tones

(Refs: Appendix I, page 114 and 116; II Banks 7, 8, 10, page 129–133)

In recent years, the notional-functional approach to language description has attracted a good deal of attention. Furthermore, the role of language as a vehicle for interpersonal communication has assumed greater significance in language studies. The model used in the present book relates these two conceptual trends in the form of the *socio-semantic unit* which combines a specified function with an attitudinal tone appropriate to the particular activity being enacted eg suggest [+ formal].

The selection of functions stems directly from the earlier specification of activities, and the attitudinal tones derive from the specified social relationships. Thus, in the example given on page 23 above, we quote for the activity, 'asking questions for clarification', two types of function, each accompanied by appropriate attitudinal tones:

Query, [+ courteous], [+ formal].
Explain, [+ rational], [+ authoritative].

Of course, there are many ways of querying (offensively, sarcastically, etc) and as many ways of explaining (patiently, curtly, etc). Thus, the language realization of the function will be greatly influenced by the selected attitudinal tones.

Little progress has yet been made in developing tests of attitudinal tones or units of meaning, though we are convinced that the attitudinal appropriacy of an utterance is often likely to be just as important as its linguistic correctness. If we test attitudinal skills by using the meta-language of social relationships, asking testees to classify samples as being explanations, verifications or prohibitions accompanied by tones such as 'convivial' and 'laudatory'[6], the artifacts of the test present more problems and difficulties than the task itself. It is also likely that a good deal of tolerance is extended by competent language users to the failure of obvious learners to hit exactly the right attitudinal key in conversation or correspondence. Nevertheless, the fewer strains put on communicative credibility, the better it will be for the learner.

Test format

Tests may be classified in three format categories, open-ended, closed-ended and restricted-response:

Open-ended tests

In open-ended tests, the testee's contribution is constrained only by the communicative task he is required to undertake. Being free to initiate, elaborate or qualify and to adopt the attitude he considers appropriate, the testee finds himself in a fairly authentic communicative setting. If he can be assessed on the basis of real-life performance and in terms of behavioural outcomes, the testing situation acquires the characteristics commended by Morrow (1977). The open-ended format also lends itself to the assessment of multiple-mode tasks, such as research and discussion, and to the probing of the mastery of the function/tone units of meaning. It can thus be seen that the open-ended format is most likely to meet our criteria of authenticity and to impart relevance and acceptability to our tests. The problem is then to ensure that we add in features to provide for comparability and economy.

Closed-ended tests

In the closed-ended test, the testee is hemmed in, not only by the constraints of the task, but also by the demands of the test procedures. In fact, most of the characteristics described by Morrow are, perforce, absent and the testee's behaviour is limited to responding without the opportunity to initiate, modify or develop and he may only select from among those options which the test deviser has put before him. The kind of communication enacted reminds one of a doctor trying to extract information from a sick man by the method – 'Nod once for yes, twice for no, and three times for don't know.' Clearly the multiple-choice test has few of the characteristics of normal communication, but it does have certain practical advantages which make it a useful component of a test system. Lacking relevance and authenticity, doubtless, but making for objectivity of scoring and economy in marking, it allows for economy and comparability. We might use it where broad indices of language mastery are required, when we wish to make a diagnosis of enabling skills, or when we wish to provide an objective check on subjective but more relevant types of assessment. Because they only provide an indirect measure of communicative performance and because of their backwash effect on teaching programmes, we may wish to use closed-ended tests for only a narrow range of purposes.

Restricted-response tests

The format of restricted response allows somewhat more latitude because it provides the testee with the opportunity actually to compose a response, but it still restricts him to the responding mode. Nevertheless, because the acceptable responses can be spelt out clearly, there is an element of objectivity in the marking, and the thorough researching of the various options needed for closed-ended tests is not necessary. Many good tests, such as the Stanford–Binet intelligence test, rely on the restricted-response format. We thus have a format which allows for some relevance, a fair amount of objectivity to achieve comparability, is generally acceptable and, at least in its construction, fairly economical.

Notes

[1] Adapted from the specification prepared by Roger Hawkey, English Language Division, British Council.
[2] Original version prepared by Shelagh Rixon, of the British Council's English

Language Teaching Institute, and later expanded for the Royal Society of Arts.

[3] Putative response = the response imagined by a writer or speaker in the absence of an immediate, overt response. Note that the non-communicative uses of language for problem-solving and abstract thinking are unlikely to pose an L2 problem and are not included in our model.

[4] Frequency is judged on a scale 1 (daily) to 4 (likely to occur less than once a month).

[5] Survival is judged from 1 (easily remedied) to 4 ('matter of life and death').

[6] These terms are taken from the Munby index of attitudinal tones (op cit).

3. The development of communicative tests

Introduction

Having systematically studied the participants' needs and specified the test content, the next step is to write the tests themselves. This is perhaps the most difficult of all the phases because it requires a combination of scientific understanding and creative writing. Making the initial needs analysis and handling test data can be carried out according to clearly defined procedures, but the test writer is expected to produce an attractive, workable, authentic set of tasks, bearing in mind the many criteria set up in the design, derived from the ten information banks and the four test characteristics already fully described.

The demands of authenticity will often conflict with the need to produce a reliable testing instrument. In the typical language test, authenticity is often abandoned in the search for reliability and economy, and the result too often is a monotonous series of linguistic manipulations only distantly related to real communicative tasks. Enabling or subsidiary skills can legitimately be the subject of testing, but they must be tested in the context of genuine operational skills, seen to be component parts of such skills and handled in as realistic a manner as possible.

One important way of providing tests with some measure of authenticity is to provide 'source material' in the form of files, booklets and tapes, so that testees may search through relevant material to solve the problems set. In a test of language for academic purposes, for example, they may be given a booklet or folder with significant texts from the discipline concerned. In a test of English for Life Sciences, a booklet may be prepared dealing with such topics as 'Antibiotic therapy', 'Inheritance', 'Lipids', 'Lactation curves', 'Nutrition', 'Correlation of Ecological studies', 'Weights and Measures' and appropriate 'Contents', 'Bibliography' and 'Index'. All these texts may be taken from standard literature and co-ordinated by an inter-disciplinary team of language and subject specialists, using as a guide to test content the modes and skills already specified.

For occupational purposes, say, for Management Studies, a folder and files may be used, with authentic materials and case-studies, tapes of briefings and excerpts from seminars; for Social Survival purposes – a folder with air schedules, guide-book material, maps, diagrams, pictures, pro-formas and instructions of various kinds, as well as tapes of news broadcasts and announcements relevant to the skills and functions specified (as in Appendix II) and in the appropriate modes.

Thus in contrast to uncontextualized multiple-choice format and non-specific cloze or comprehension passages, the content of source materials is highly relevant to communication in the discipline or occupation concerned, and reflects the common requirement of searching through lots of information, using reference techniques, in order to solve the tasks and answer the questions given. The aim is to assess communicative proficiency in the subject concerned, not to test specific knowledge of it. Thus it would not be assumed that the testee knew that 1 fl oz = 28 ml or that 1 dram = 480 g. Such information, if essential for performing a task, would be provided with the source material.

In the following pages we confine ourselves to the broad outlines of test development, with selected examples, dealing first with tests focused on the single modes of reading, listening, writing and speaking (remembering the reservations about the incompleteness of these categories), and then the multimode activities of oral interaction (L+S), note-taking (L+W), research (R+W) and the complete, integrated mode (L+R+S+W).

Single-focus tests

Tests of reading

The major focus on reading and understanding a text suggests keeping to the closed-ended or restricted-response formats. For a student wishing to undertake a course in Business Studies in English (the participant in the specification in Appendix I) here are tests for a sample of skills, using the text *Demand and supply* as a source.

Demand and supply

Having made these assumptions about conditions in a competitive market, we must now make some assumptions about the nature of the forces at work in that market – demand and supply. So far as demand by buyers is concerned, it seems reasonable to think that there will be some very high prices at which no buyer will purchase anything, and some very low prices at which all buyers will buy large quantities of cotton. Between these limits, the lower the price is the more cotton will be bought. For buyers who were previously unable to afford any cotton will be able to do so when its price falls and *vice versa*. Similarly, it is reasonable to assume that when prices are very high sellers will be only too keen to sell as much cotton as they can, while conditions remain good. Again, when prices are low, sellers will tend to hold back their supplies in the hope that prices will rise. At intermediate prices, varying amounts of cotton will be sold. The higher the price is, the greater the amount of cotton offered by sellers is likely to be. For, the higher the price, the more anxious sellers will be to dispose of their supplies while prices remain high.

We shall therefore assume that the amounts of cotton supplied and demanded at various hypothetical prices are as shown in Table 1 below.

Assuming that the demand and supply schedules are as shown in Table 1, our assumption that competition is keen means that a price of £3.50 per bale will be reached before the market closes. For this is the only

Table 1: Demand and supply schedules

Price per bale	Demand schedule (at this price buyers will take (bales))	Supply schedule (at this price sellers will offer (bales))
£6.50	–	120 000
£5.50	20 000	100 000
£4.50	40 000	80 000
£3.50	60 000	60 000
£2.50	80 000	40 000
£1.50	100 000	20 000
£0.50	120 000	–

price at which the amount demanded is equal to the amount supplied. Only at this price can *all* those wishing to sell and to buy *at any one price* be satisfied.

If the market price is above £3.50, more cotton will be offered by sellers than is demanded by buyers and the tendency will be for the price to fall. Those sellers who are unable to dispose of their supplies at the existing price will begin to make price reductions in the hope of attracting custom. As the price falls, amount demanded will increase and amount supplied will decline in the way shown in Table 1 until, at the price of £3.50, all the sellers who are willing to sell will be able to find purchasers for their cotton. Similarly, if the price is below £3.50 a bale, the amount of cotton demanded will exceed the amount supplied and the price of cotton will tend to rise. For there will be many unsatisfied buyers at any price below £3.50. While they would be only too glad to buy at a lower price if possible, they will be prepared to see the price rise rather than go away empty-handed. When the price has risen to £3.50, all the buyers who are prepared to buy at the price will be satisfied.

Only at a price of £3.50 a bale will there be no tendency for the price to change. Only at this price will there be no unsatisfied buyers or sellers who are prepared to see prices alter rather than go away without having bought or sold any cotton. Consequently, it is only when the price is £3.50 a bale that the price will remain stable at a given level. This price at which the amounts demanded and supplied are equal is known in technical language as the *equilibrium price*. At this price the forces of demand and supply are balanced, or in equilibrium. It is called an equilibrium price because price settles down, or comes to rest, at this level. . . .

Figure 8: *Skill 52.* **Transcoding written information through completing a graph.**

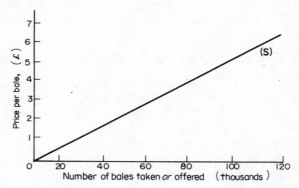

(*Question 1*) Refer to the *Demand and supply* schedule table given in the text and draw the missing curve in the graph below:

(*Answer*: a line drawn from the top left corner to the bottom right corner and marked (**D**). The response could also be elicited by choosing one of a number of alternative curves, in a multiple-choice format.)

Skill 51: Transcoding information by converting a table into writing

(*Question 2*) Complete the following sentences using information given in the *Demand and supply schedules*:

At a price of £4.50 per bale, buyers will take . . . . bales.
(*Answer*: 40,000)
At a price of £1.50 per bale, buyers will take . . . . bales.
(*Answer*: 100,000)
At a price of £2.50 per bale, sellers will offer . . . . bales.
(*Answer*: 40,000)

As the price per bale rises, the number demanded will fall, and the number . . . .   (*Answer*: offered will rise)

Note: In none of the above test items are the responses wholly deducible from language features. One might therefore ask: Are we testing the language of our testees? The answer is that the primary purpose is to test their communicative skills in settings closely related to those of the authentic task. Language usage, clearly a component of such skills, is therefore a testing focus, but it is not the only one.

Skill 46.2: Scanning to obtain specifically required information on more than one point

(*Question 3*) At what price will the price of cotton remain stable, and what kind of market must exist for this statement to be true? (*Answer*: £3.50, a competitive market.)
What is the unit in which cotton is sold?
− alternatively −
What is a bale?
(*Answer*: the bale *or* a unit for measuring cotton.)

Skill 45.1: Skimming to obtain gist of passage

This skill is probably best tested by multiple-choice items.
(*Question 4*) Which of the following most adequately describes the topic of the passage on 'Demand and supply'?

(A) Advice on how to buy and sell cotton.
(B) The operation of demand and supply forces in a competitive market.
(C) The establishment of the equilibrium price in a competitive market.

(*Answer*: B. Although each of the other options is dealt with in the passage, option B is the most comprehensive or adequate.)

Skill 39.7: Distinguishing the main idea from supporting details by differentiating proposition from argument

(*Question 5*) Arrange the following three unpunctuated word groups to fit into a meaningful pattern: Because – and because–, then –.

(A) in any transaction the buying price and the selling price must be the same
(B) the price must settle down at the equilibrium price of £3.50
(C) at any other price the market will not be in equilibrium.

(*Answer*: Because A and because C, then B.)

Skill 32 (1, 3, 4, 6): Understanding relations between parts of text through the grammatical cohesion devices of reference, substitution, ellipsis and logical connectors

(*Question 6*) In the following passage you are given three options at certain places. Choose the word or phrase which fits best into the passage:

Our first point is that to appreciate the clarity of the

$\left.\begin{array}{l}\text{above}\\\text{given}\\\text{written}\end{array}\right\}$ passage on 'Demand and supply',

we should read $\left.\begin{array}{l}\text{diligently}\\\text{another}\\\text{a passage}\end{array}\right\}$ in which clear examples have been given.

One passage is easy to understand, the other is $\left\{\begin{array}{l}\text{as well.}\\\text{unintelligible.}\\\text{not easy.}\end{array}\right.$

We can $\left\{\begin{array}{l}\text{there}\\\text{also}\\\text{thus}\end{array}\right.$ appreciate that good examples increase clarity.

Our $\left\{\begin{array}{l}\text{third}\\\text{second}\\\text{first}\end{array}\right.$ point is much more complex, ... etc.

(*Answers*: above, a passage, unintelligible, thus, second.)

Skill 30.6: Understanding relations between parts of a text through the lexical cohesion device of set

(*Question* 7) Arrange the following words into four columns representing (1) Units of measurement (2) Commercial products (3) Economic trends (4) Economic forces.
pound[1], cotton[2], increase[3], demand[4], reduction[3], pence[1], cocoa[2], supply[4], oil[2], profit[4], tons[1], decrease[3].
(Preferred grouping indicated above after each word.)

Skill 26: Understanding the communicative value of a text in respect of the micro-functions, — six categories listed in Appendix 1, 9, 26/27, page 116–118

The implications of this skill category, which brings together a whole range of micro-functions with their linguistic realizations in the service of a language skill, are very wide. Furthermore, there is the added complication that communicative value may exist without explicit indicators. As an example, the function 'order' may be realized with explicit indicators:

'Please, turn the light off', or without,
'That light's been left on again'.

In academic discourse a parallel would be:

'Marshall's theory of consumer demand is basically inadequate'. (Explicit).
'Marshall's theory of consumer demand is admirable as far as it goes'. (Not so explicit)

The nature of test items will depend on the sophistication of the testees; if they can be assumed to understand such terms as 'approve', 'complain', 'advocate' and so on, the items can test directly using the meta-language of functional description as follows:

(*Question* 8) Match the following phrases with the functions given:

(A) approve   (a) Why don't you try aspirins?
(B) complain   (b) I have never said such a thing.

(C) advocate   (c) There is much to be said for this idea.
(D) deny   (d) These files are always so untidy.

(*Answer*: Ac, Bd, Ca, Db).

The mastery of these functions, with or without explicit indicators, can be tested in a less artificial manner in spoken or written dialogue.

Skill 24: Understanding conceptual meaning ie quantity, definiteness, comparison, time, means, cause, result

A significant language skill category, with wide scope for test writing depending on the delicacy with which the skills have to be tested. Items may be presented in context and even in discrete sentences, although there is a danger of ambiguity and lack of authenticity in the latter format.

Concept	*Language realizations (contrastive)*
Quantity	all/few; many/much; each/every; any/more.
Definiteness	the tiger/a tiger; the food/food; this/that.
Comparison	more than/as much as; enough/too; so much that; the more the . . .; little/less; better than x can; better than usual.
Time	habitual/occurring; formerly/for some time; since/used to.
Means	with a/by means of.
Cause	because of/through.
Result	(+) so that/in case; provided that/unless/but for; (−) even though/in spite of

The use of selective cloze techniques, matching and specially-framed comprehension tests can probe this key language area. In the following example the deleted words are inserted in brackets. A list of alternative acceptable words may be drawn up.

(*Question 9*) Insert one word in each of the blank spaces in this passage (in this sample test, the missing words are supplied).
Five principal types of social group structure nucleus were identified by the author:

(1) The (*most*) elementary and clear-cut nucleus was the mutual first choice of two or (*more*) individuals amongst themselves.

(2) Non-mutual choices capable of being represented by chains of (*any*) number of individuals.

(3) The configuration described as a 'star', (*resulting*) from the clustering of a larger number of choices around a (*single*) individual.

(4) A grouping around a powerful as (*opposed*) to a popular individual. A popular individual may have a large number of choices but, (*in*) (*spite*) of this, he might have very little influence (*owing*) to the limited contacts of his admirers.

(5) These are isolated individuals chosen by nobody or (*few*) others. Such individuals (*are*) frequently maladjusted. The (*reason*) for this is that they are cut off from the currents of feeling which (*influence*) the behaviour of the group.

Skill 20: Understanding explicitly-stated information

We will not exemplify this particular skill in test form as it is so frequently handled in conventional test formats, usually by multiple-choice or short answer item types.

Other skills and activities

The examples given above have been those considered suitable for testing English in an academic programme and drawing on the texts and skills used by a student. In everyday social interaction, such as in the situations envisaged in Appendix II, there will be a change of emphasis in texts and skills. Specified activities giving rise to authentic reading tests would be:

Event 4: Travel
Activity 4, understand road signs and symbols.
Activity 5, study time-tables and schedules.

Event 5: Obtaining medical attention
Activity 4, read medical forms and documents.

Event 7: Using media
Activity 1, read TV and radio schedules and announcements.

Event 8: Studying for interest and information
Activity 2, use a simplified dictionary.
Activity 3, use basic reference books.
Activity 10, research for information.

Event 9: Reading for pleasure
Activity 1, read news headlines and simple reports.
Activity 4, read magazine articles, editorials and correspondence.
Activity 5, read full novels, and poems.

A run-down of skills, taken from the Munby list (*op cit* pp 176–218) and suitable for testing would be:

Skill number	*Abbreviated skill description*
51/52	Transcoding.
45/46	Skimming and scanning.
44	Basic reference skills.
43	Reducing the text.
39	Distinguishing the main idea.
35	Recognizing indicators in discourse.
34	Interpreting text by going outside it. (A strategy of considerable relevance in a strange cultural environmentment.)
30/31	Understanding relations through lexical and grammatical cohesion devices.
26	Understanding communicative value (especially *without* explicit indicators).
24	Understanding conceptual meaning.
17	Recognizing the script of the target language.

Coupled with these skills is the recognition of language realizations of the functions (Munby, 1978 pp 136–139), especially:

– the personalized functions (category 1);
– judgement and evaluation (category 3);

– suasion (category 4);
– formulaic communication (category 7).

We have gone into a certain amount of detail in the exemplification of tests of reading to show how the taxonomy of language skills may be drawn upon for testing both broad communicative skills and subordinate language skills. The following sections refer the reader to the above examples to be re-applied in the appropriate modes.

[One general piece of advice for test writers is to have available a subject expert when writing and editing the texts. It is very easy for language specialists to mishandle or misunderstand terminology and discourse in other disciplines, especially those relating to Science and Technology.]

Tests of listening

Activities which lend themselves to tests of listening, or at least to tests with a major component of listening, are illustrated with reference to the Social Survival specification in Appendix II.5 page 124ff:

Social interaction Understand instructions on how to operate equipment (eg radio)
Visiting places of interest Understand descriptions given by a guide or friend.
Travel Understand spoken description of maps or diagrams.
Medical attention Understand directions for treatment.
Using the media Understand TV and radio news and announcements. Follow film, play, TV series or documentaries, taking calls on telephone
Studying for interest Understand talks and debates.

These are the activities which the learner may well be expected to take part in, so they will form a nucleus of testing situations, always remembering that we can, if needed, test not only the broader language skills but also the enabling skills of which they are made up.

Examples of listening tests

The following is a role-playing situation. The testee has been asked to wait for a telephone call for someone who has gone away for a time. His task is to understand the message and pass it on when that person returns.

'You are visiting a friend's house. He is expecting a telephone call, but has had to go out for half an hour. Listen to the telephone call so that you can answer your friend's questions about it when he returns.'

— Brr-brr. Brr-brr. Brr-brr.
— Hello. Is David in? No. All right, will you please take a message for him from Rita? This is it: (*taped message follows*)

either
You wish to leave a note for David as you have to leave shortly. Choose the words or phrases in this written message which tell David about the telephone call.

'Dear David,

I have just $\left.\begin{array}{l} \text{arrived} \\ \text{sent} \\ \text{taken} \end{array}\right\}$ a phone call from $\left.\begin{array}{l} \text{Rence} \\ \text{Rita} \\ \text{Ghita} \end{array}\right\}$. She wonders if

you would like to go to $\left.\begin{array}{l} \text{visit the zoo} \\ \text{the cinema} \\ \text{call round} \end{array}\right\}$ this evening at about $\begin{array}{l} 5 \\ 6 \\ 7 \end{array}$ o'clock.

Can you ring her back before $\left.\begin{array}{l} 3.30 \\ 4.30 \\ 5.30 \end{array}\right\}$ and let her know. Her number

just now is $\left.\begin{array}{l} 387\ 2496 \\ 287\ 3597 \\ 377\ 3494 \end{array}\right\}$

or
Write a note to David saying who called, what she wanted to know, when to ring her back and giving her present phone number.

Another type of test item is the combining of listening with a diagram, table, picture or sequence of pictures. In Event 7 (Appendix II) is specified the understanding of TV and radio news and announcements, so the evening's TV schedule may be presented as a table and announcements may be made which will interpret or modify the published schedule.

TV programmes: Sunday 5th March
1745   News. Programme announcements.
1800   Nationwide – topical news.
1900   The Waltons – domestic drama.
1930   The Rockford File – detective series.
2000   Casablanca – war-time film.
2130   Panorama – events of the week.
2200   News at Ten.
2230   International Football.
2330   News summary.
2340   Close down.

Areas for questions:

– insertion of special 10-minute feature; implications for later programmes;
– playing of headlines of the three news programmes and spotting the
  differences;
– announcement of European Cup football scores and discussion of
  prospects of teams;
– extracting main points of a news item.

The coverage of language skills for listening will proceed in a manner rather like that demonstrated in the examples of reading test items, by tracing a path from the broader, operational skills down through the narrower sub-skills involved in the successful achievement of a communicative goal. As an extreme example, it may be thought useful to test the ability to discriminate between the initial consonants p and b. If a case had been established for testing such a microscopic skill, the test format should involve the tackling of a genuine communicative problem where the solution lies in the particular phonemic contrast under discussion.

Testing of writing

The closest approach to a single-mode writing test is the imaginative essay or the description of a picture, object and the enacted or remembered event. In terms of the diagram in Figure 6, the writing may be a delayed response to some stimulus, and written as a letter or note in the expectation of an immediate response. In a test setting, the writer addresses himself, in effect, to the examiner whom he imagines to be likely to scrutinize his creations.

Contexts for plausible writing tasks are readily available in the two specifications in the appendices. Let us extract first from the Business Studies activities:

7.1: Taking notes that can be re-constituted.
7.4: Selecting, sorting and sequencing information for reports or essays.
7.4: Writing factual accounts of theories, practices and trends.
7.4: Writing evaluative reports and essays on theories, practices and procedures.
7.6: Discussing (in writing) matters observed during industrial and commercial visits.

From the Social English specification we could extract suitable activities from the activities listed below.

Event 3: Write a letter ordering domestic goods. Acknowledging receipt of goods and making arrangements for payment. Completing hire purchase forms.
Event 8: Write reports on a study topic (hobby).
Event 10: Write a diary entry of personal report of a visit.
Event 11: Write a letter to ask an official for clarification of a ruling about student accommodation.

It can be seen that the particular test items devised all occur naturally in the daily life of a student or visitor. The amount of stimulus for the writing can vary from a brief instruction – 'Write a critical report of your visit to the Kingston Industrial Estate' – to an elaborate scenario presented in the form of a file of correspondence which the testee is required to digest so as to solve the particular problem under discussion.

Another type of stimulus is the non-verbal presentation through a graph or picture. And in all cases there is the option of a fully written-out essay or an abbreviated presentation in the form of notes or headings.

There are also interesting possibilities, short of the free-writing examples given above, in re-ordering chunks of test to give the best temporal or logical sequence, the picking out of a coherent sequence of sentences from a mixture of relevant and irrelevant statements, and the building up of a full discourse by selecting given sentences and inserting one's own where there are gaps in the text being assembled.

The language skills to be tested may be taken from Appendix I as follows:

Skill 51: Conversion of a graph into writing.
Skill 50: Organizing information in expository language (especially presentation of reports).
Skill 47 — 49: Initiating, maintaining and terminating written discourse.
Skill 41: Co-ordinating related information and tabulating information for comparison and contrast.
Skills 31 + 33: Expressing relations between parts of a text through lexical and grammatical cohesion devices.

The main problem in testing writing has always been that of assessing the merit of the work presented. However, as shown below in the section dealing with assessment scales, the amount of detail now available from the needs analyses will give the opportunity of using both the time-honoured 'quick, subjective rating' system and a set of ratings based on performance criteria for writing. (See Appendix III, Scales 4, 5, 6). It is commonly accepted that the reliability of an assessment of writing increases with the number of topics and the number of independent assessments made.

Tests of speaking

It is difficult to discover instances of single-mode speaking activities. In practice, speech is part of an interactive chain and it is unreal to expect to be able to test it as an isolated language activity. The Business Studies analysis in Appendix I, for example, includes the activities – 'asking for clarification in a lecture' and 'discussing topics during and after industrial visits' – essentially listen-speak activities, the spoken aspects depending on the comprehension of the contributions of the other speaker or speakers.

The Social English analysis, Appendix II, includes the activities – 'making spoken complaints', 'making orders by telephone', 'complaining or appreciating in a restaurant' and 'discussing one's needs with an official' – and it is clear that the development of the situation will demand listening comprehension just as much as spoken proficiency. There may be learners who will have demands for continuous speech, such as lecturers or politicians, who are by custom given a fair amount of time to develop their thesis with the minimum of interruption from their audience, and in such cases a reasonably authentic test of spoken language could be devised. But these are comparatively rare. If we apply the criteria of potential needs and authenticity, we are not often likely to require pure tests of spoken proficiency, but rather a mixed-mode test of oral interaction.

Testing techniques which minimize the interactive aspects of oral production include those concerned with:

– information given to the testee in his mother tongue;
– description of past experiences or technical aspects of the testee's own professional field;
– transcoding information presented in diagrams/tables/graphs/pictures into speech;
– describing an event which has just been enacted;
– presenting a mini-lecture on a topic within the testee's experience.

In these ways the focus is on the mode being tested. We must, however, question the authenticity of tests narrowly focused on spoken performance.

Mixed mode tests

Oral Interaction (L+S)

Communicative needs analysis suggests that oral interaction

(L+S) is the most commonly-encountered type. The separate testing of speaking and listening runs the risk of failing to allow for the key characteristics of communication – that one must interact, initiate and develop coherently a theme of which one only controls a portion. Of course, one must be able to listen with understanding and to speak intelligibly, but oral interaction brings in a completely new element, that of constructive interplay with unpredictable stimuli.

There have been several attempts to devise standardized methods of assessing oral proficiency, but they have run up against the familiar dilemma of the conflicting demands of authenticity and scientific measurement. There is, for example, the ingenious method of presenting one half of a conversation on tape in a language laboratory and recording the testee's responses. But this one-sided dialogue is not genuinely interactive, because the stimulus voice, previously scripted and recorded, continues on its own path regardless of the responses of the testee, who is thus denied any real role in guiding the conversation or in initiating themes. Other attempts at oral assessment have been based on the reading of one half of a dialogue by the examiner and free responses by the testee, and even a play-reading type of test for which the examiner and the testee read to each other their respective portions of the dialogue. It is difficult to see how these 'dialogue of the deaf' formats can produce anything approaching genuine oral interaction.

However, given the authentic settings provided by graphic and oral source materials such as those described at the beginning of this chapter, and the likelihood that the testee can play a reasonably authentic role (including that of himself!) the chances of authentic oral interaction are increased.

A further measure to increase authenticity is to arrange for interlocuters to represent, to some extent at least, the varied social relationships the testee is likely to be involved in. In the normal interview, the relationship is mainly that of inquisitor-victim, with a strong pattern of dominance and lack of social cohesion not likely to be representative of future interactions. The interactive possibilities may be diversified by putting the assessor in the background and bringing in a non-assessing, native speaker as role player. We can also introduce other testees, to provide multi-directional social relationships. The need for extra personnel for the interview is to some extent offset by the economy of assessing several testees at one time.

Testing must produce a reasonably consistent assessment of the testee's performance. For what it is worth, there is a certain amount of evidence that, if assessors are given suitable training and guidance, judgements of oral performance can achieve a fair level of inter-rater and intra-rater reliability. Assessment scales using overall impression descriptions, as well as detailed breakdowns of various significant aspects of performance (such as those in Appendix III), can form the basis of reasonably consistent assessment. As it happens, earlier scales have given priority to usage/language aspects of performance, high-lighting vocabulary, grammar and pronunciation features rather than the effectiveness and appropriacy of communication. Our own scales, however, give priority to discourse and communicative features and are based on the ten performance criteria described in Chapter 2 above (see also Appendix III).

One valuable supplement to the interview-test assessment of oral proficiency is the rating, based on everyday observation, by a teacher who knows the testee well. Ratings or rankings by such a person, when scaled by a common criterion, are likely to be both reliable and valid.

To summarize, the assessment of oral interaction is an extremely difficult business and will be most effectively achieved by establishing authentic interactive settings, by drawing on carefully specified topics, by using several types of interlocuter, by the use of detailed, communicatively-based criteria and by using the ratings of an experienced teacher acquainted with the testee. At present, oral assessment cannot be other than a time-consuming and troublesome business and many problems of validity and reliability still remain unresolved.

Note-taking (L + W)

A distinction is drawn between note-taking from an *oral source* and note-making from a *graphic source*. Moreover, it is not the form of the notes themselves that is important, but the ability of their writer to re-constitute them in a satisfactory form. It is quite common for the notes themselves to be untidy, and even unintelligible to an outsider, but perfectly meaningful to the note-taker himself. The pay-off, then, is not the notes themselves but the completeness and accuracy of the presentation made on the basis of the notes.

The stimulus may be an authentic lecture or experimental demonstration on a relevant topic, during which the testee may take notes to be written up, preferably after an interval, to the satisfaction of an experienced assessor. The rating is made in terms both of their content and of communicative adequacy according to an appropriate rating scale. The face-to-face lecture procedure may be replaced by video- or audio-tape recordings in the interests of standardized presentation. If the notes are to be re-constructed orally (L+W+S), testee performance can be rated according to an oral assessment scale.

Research (R+W)

The term research may be interpreted rather broadly to include not only the activities of the academic student in writing an essay or thesis, but also the day-to-day information collection of, say, a tourist who wishes to write a report or even a letter to a friend.

The content of the test will be drawn from the specified activities and topics, the stimulus will be reference material provided, the response a report of a given type and the rating based on a communicative writing scale (as in Appendix III). Multiplying the number of topics treated and the number of independent assessments made will increase the reliability of the ratings.

Complete, integrated tests (L+R+S+W)

A complete test of communicative performance involves the integrated operation of all four modes. Such a test approaches most nearly the authenticity of genuine situations, whilst providing opportunities for use of objective items in context and for appropriately devised rating scales.

Information may be presented to the testees orally (by voice or by audio- or video-tape) and graphically (by printed instructions or source materials such as those already described). Supplementary information may be available on tape and through reference material, and the tester will be empowered to provide certain information on request. Consultation between testees, if appropriate to the future setting, may also be permitted. The circumstances of the testing will thus be rather similar to the traditional procedures used by management and military assessment boards, except that the focus is now on communicative proficiency rather than on professional competence.

The overt responses of the testees will be very diverse. Orally, they can provide information to the supervisor, or record it on tape; or they can present information to peer groups and be prepared to defend their own findings or points of view. Graphically, they may be required to give information on pro-formas or make synopses, comparative comments and summary reports in free-writing format. A judicious balance between subjective and objective assessment of performance, with the possibility of diagnostic comment, is valuable for further tutorial purposes.

As a measure of economy, only those testees who have met certain criteria, or performed to a certain level in easily administered paper-and-pencil tests, might be given the complete, integrated test mode. Alternatively, the tests can be phased in successively more difficult stages with progressive elimination of candidates according to performance. The side effects of this type of testing on teaching programmes must be extremely healthy, providing for the congruence of needs, programmes and tests which we have recommended earlier.

Trial application of tests

When we have designed our test system and realized it in actual items or tasks, we are in a position to try out the test instrument with a suitable pre-test sample. Because of the insistence on detailed specification, the tasks we expect the pre-testing to do are essentially different from those of pre-testing of less rigorously designed test instruments. What we want to know is, in effect, whether or not the items are testing those communicative areas we intended them to. In multiple-choice formats, we will want to know whether the distractors are working in the right direction; in open-ended formats, we will want to know if the test situations are eliciting the appropriate skills and that the assessments possess relevance and stability. In restricted-response formats, we will want to inject into the final instrument the optimum balance of relevance, acceptability, comparability and economy.

Language bands

In order to discuss further the nature of the pre-test sample of testees, it is now necessary to outline a device which is central to all our testing operations, namely the *nine-point language band* system, a framework presenting in grid form a series of nine performance levels (as shown in Figure 9) and ten language performance variables (as shown in Appendix III)

There is a long and honourable tradition of rating scales of this kind. A well-known example is the proficiency rating scale developed in America in the 1950s by the Foreign Service Institute, effectively a ten-point scale (with five main levels and five interlevels) ranging from native-speaker equivalence down to a very elementary level of performance, approximately representing the range provided by our own rating system.

As there are few demands to assess the language performance of expert users, the top level, Band 9, is really a notional category put in as a ceiling, and we do not assume a continuum from Band 8 to Band 9. However, as no-one, not even a native speaker, is equally at home in all fields of knowledge, from Psychiatry to Atomic Physics, there will be many cases in ESP testing when a special non-native speaker will return a higher score than a native speaker who is not a specialist. Indeed, it has been found that educated native-speakers, especially if they are no longer young and flexible, have experienced great difficulty in completing a study skills test in Technology, whereas a young non-native speaking Engineer can cope with it with perfect facility. In ESP what is being tested is not a general language

Figure 9: The nine-point language band system

Band	Performance levels	L–S	L	R–W	R	AV		
9	Expert							9
8	Very good							8
7	Good							7
6	Competent							6
5	Modest							5
4	Marginal							4
3	Extremely limited							3
2	Intermittent							2
1/0	Non-user							1

mastery, but the ability to perform appropriate communicative operations requiring specified language skills and insights in specified
subject areas. This does not mean that our primary purpose is to test a
knowledge of particular disciplines.

Again, it is rarely needed to test non-users of a language (no doubt a
singularly unrewarding exercise!), so we do not describe the non-user
in Band 1/0, but start discriminating performance levels at Band 2. For
working purposes, there is effectively a seven-level system, Bands 2 to
8, with a 'ceiling' and a 'floor' as polarity markers.

The numbers 1–9 and the shorthand labels for the types of performer
at each level are, of course, much too unspecific to form a basis for
assessments of communicative performance. They are convenient,
however, for the decision-maker whose task is essentially to match the

performance profile of an individual with the requirement profile of a particular job, for which purpose too much detail merely becomes a block to communication. But the language tester will need much greater and more scientific statements of performance levels. For this purpose we may use a more elaborate set of definitions, such as those shown in Appendix III, which describe under conventional headings typical performances of EAP testees at various levels. The tests in this example used authentic texts from a number of subjects and disciplines (Architecture, Science, Engineering and Arts), so that the performances were specific to students familiar with the bases of a particular discipline. Such guidance is handy for the assessment of writing and oral interaction, especially if accompanied by photostat or taped examples.

Nevertheless, because these handy specifications are rather arbitrary in their selection of performance examples, we have devised a full specification procedure, exemplified in Appendix III, which applies a consistent set of 10 performance criteria to certain Band levels.

The first four criteria indicate features of a written or spoken text: *size, complexity, range* and *speed*; the remaining six criteria refer to characteristics of the testee's language performance: *flexibility, accuracy, appropriacy, independence, repetition* and *hesitation*. For our highest levels of performance, we would present our testee with communicative situations of maximum difficulty regarding test size, complexity, range and speed and judge his response most meticulously in respect of flexibility, accuracy, appropriacy, independence, repetition and hesitation.

In the particular project for which the above specification was prepared, the *target level* performance was at Band 7 ('good user'), where the learner could be expected to cope with the daily demands of living and working in an English-speaking environment; the *basic level* performance would be at the bottom of Band 4, and the *intermediate level* about the middle of Band 5, respectively 'marginal' and 'modest user' levels.

The retention of the extreme levels, 1 and 9, is recommended because this will allow us along the same scale to register performances in, say, overseas primary schools (Levels 1 and 2) as well as in English-speaking secondary schools (Levels 7–9) where basic competence in English must be matched by a knowledge of Science and the tools of scientific communication.

This description of the nine-point language band system has so far concentrated on the levels as represented by the horizontal rows in Figure 9. It is also necessary to examine the vertical columns to see what variables are being described. One option is to plot in the usual listen-read-speak-write 'skills', with a final average performance rating. Another is to use the multiple-mode variables described in Chapter 3 (oral interaction, note-taking, research and integrated modes). Also being explored is the devising of task-based focuses and plotting in performance at appropriate levels. These focuses could, in a Science course, be:

- carrying out instructions in a lab;
- writing up the results of an experiment;
- defending conclusions from an experiment;
- searching for references in the library;
- reading and interpreting a scientific article.

Assessment would be based either on performance in tasks of increasing difficulty in each of the above areas or on descriptions of varying qualities of response to the same task, or even on a mixing of these two procedures. Alternatively, a performance scale could be built up, such as the Stanford–Binet intelligence scale of performance, appropriate to different age or sophistication levels. All the above approaches are being developed and only time will tell which type will best suit the various assessment situations. In any event, these developments should contribute to the achievement of test relevance, acceptability and economy.

Standard 'L' scores

However, we still have to meet the demands of comparability or stability of the ratings given, a problem to be solved by the careful devising of performance scales, the provision of sample performances judged by competent assessors to represent various levels, the training of raters and constant monitoring by teams of judges. Rating stability may also be provided by scaling subjective judgements upon objectively-derived test scores. This introduces the standardized language scores, referred to as 'L' scores. In, for example, a multiple-choice or restricted-response language test of 40 items, in which a testee scores 27 correct responses, it cannot immediately be said whether this raw score represents a good or a poor performance. In other words, raw scores on objective tests mean little of themselves and have to be converted into meaningful terms through a transformation of some kind.

To accomplish this conversion, the objective raw scores of a group of testees are compared with a rating of their performances on one or more of the language performance scales; perhaps a writing or an interview scale. The first stage of the conversion, based on the assumption that performance in one language task will broadly relate to performance in another, is to plot the raw scores on the objective test against the criterion-referenced rating on the chosen task, and to construct a conversion table. Given a sample of 100 testees, the top writing rating would be plotted against the top raw score, then the 10th, 30th, 50th, 70th, 90th and bottom ratings plotted similarly against the corresponding raw scores. This would result in the tables and their graphic representation as in Figure 10 a, b and c below:

Figure 10a: Conversion of raw to 'L' scores

Student ranking/100	Writing assessment	Raw score/40
Top	7·5	38
10th	7·0	33
30th	6·0	30
50th	5·5	24
70th	4·5	19
90th	3·0	14
Bottom	2·0	7

Figure 10b: Graph of assessment – score relationship

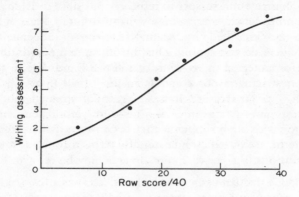

Figure 10c: Conversion table for raw 'L' scores

Raw score	'L' score	Raw score	'L' score
40	78 (or above)	19	42
39	76	18	40
38	75	17	38
37	73	16	36
36	71	15	34
35	70	14	32
34	68	13	30
33	66	12	28
32	65	11	26
31	63	10	23
30	62	9	21
29	60	8	20
28	59	7	18
27	58	6	17
26	57	5	16
25	56	4	15
24	54	3	14
23	52	2	13
22	49	1	12
21	47	0	11 (or below)
20	45		

On the basis of the original assumption of an appreciable relationship between objective and subjective tests, we may now provide an interim standard score for each of the raw scores from 0 to 40, eg a raw score of 30 is now estimated to be an 'L' score of 62. The 'L' score corresponds to the rating multiplied by 10, so that 62 would approximate performance at the bottom of the 6th Band, 'fairly competent user'. A raw score of 19 converts to an 'L' score of 42, ie, in the 4th Band, 'marginal user'. It must again be stressed that the conversion estimate is an interim one and should be checked by comparison with other ratings as they become available and ultimately by long-term, follow-up validation. Thus, by a process of successive approximations, the conversion estimates may be refined.

Figure 11 gives actual examples of the 'L' scores of five students on a language improvement programme, with 'L' scores on six tests and the

Figure 11: Examples of students' 'L' scores

Tests 1–6

Student			1	2	3	4	5	6	Av	Final rating
Number	Initial									
30	MQ	a.	70	53	37	53	60	55	55	A
		b.	85	78	80	75	70	80	78	
26	FF	a.	37	50	33	34	40	45	40	B
		b.	62	78	56	55	63	65	63	
14	SA	a.	46	32	21	53	44	40	39	C
		b.	60	65	62	58	50	60	59	
27	MM	a.	20	30	23	32	36	30	29	D
		b.	42	60	54	42	58	50	51	
37	MN	a.	18	29	18	22	30	10	21	E
		b.	26	36	25	33	36	30	31	

Note: the first score (a) was gained on the student's arrival on the course, the second score (b) was gained seven months later. The average 'L' score improvement is 20 points or 2 Bands during the course, a progress rate of approximately 200 hours per band.

mean of those scores, with an independent tutor rating from A (judged linguistically competent to cope with studies) to E (judged quite unable to cope with studies on language grounds).

This example illustrates that 'L' scores are much more meaningful than the original raw scores as they can be interpreted by reference to band descriptions. After two or three approximations both 'L' scores and rating system could be refined, linking together the relevance and acceptability of the ratings and the precision and comparability of the objective scores and giving a language performance profile for individual testees.

Item analysis

We have gone into some detail in describing the banding system because of its importance to item analysis procedures. One of the great drawbacks of some commonly-used procedures for item analysis, which rely on internal criteria such as the contrasting responses of the high scorers and low scorers of the test, is that they tend to reject items which do not conform in nature to the other items of the test. The procedures are therefore to some extent incestuous, leading to the successive rejection on non-conformist items, however relevant to needs they might be, to produce a homogeneous test, possibly irrelevant to the purposes it is intended to serve.

In the band analysis procedure, however, discrimination indices are derived from the performances of different levels of testee or criterion person, using the proportion of testees selecting the various options as a map to plot the discrimination value of each item, as exemplified in Figures 12 and 13.

Broadening the basis of criterion groups of persons reduces the danger of incestuous item selection and relates the item to much wider performance criteria. The result is a more robust test, more likely to reflect broad language level features than the internal characteristics of any single test. Criterion testees for the analysis must, however, have fairly regular profiles, otherwise the item analyses will lack clarity. Another useful feature of the band analysis procedure is the indication not only of overall discrimination and difficulty, but of the particular

Figure 12: Sample item analysis sheet

Item 32: 'Therefore' in line 7 is equivalent to –
    (A) naturally; (B) obviously; (C) *consequently*; (D) in addition.

Band	Option				
	A	B	Ⓒ	D	φ
9					
8					
7	–	–	100	–	–
6	–	37	63	–	–
5	–	37	50	–	12
4	25	12	12	–	50
3	37	–	0	12	50
2					
1					
% Av	12	17	45	2	23

levels at which these characteristics work best. With an irregular item profile, the flattest parts of the curve indicate the best discrimination areas. Thus, we could choose combinations of items which discriminate at certain bands according to our operational needs.

It should be noted again that the trial of test materials, the banding of testees and the analysis of items is a recursive process requiring several phases before acceptable precision is likely to be achieved.

Test validation

Although our item analysis procedures provide an element of validation in that items are analysed by the responses of criterion groups of testees, the normal processes of validation are still available.

First, performance on the new tests can be immediately compared with performance on existing tests and on ratings of performance by competent judges. However, one should exercise caution in such concurrent validation and try to assess how far the bases on which the existing tests have been designed are compatible with those of the

Figure 13

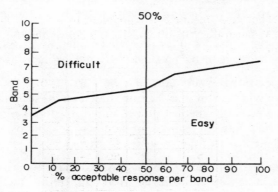

Difficulty: 45%

Discrimination: good in Bands 4, 5 and 6
(Chi-square and contingency co-efficients may also be used)

Comments: 50% of testees in Bands 4 and 5 not respond.
Distractor D not working very well. Probably as it does not fit in formally ('in addition').

Verdict: Probably useful item for 4 to 6 discrimination but examine and alter option D.

communicative tests. The more divergent the bases, the less relevant will be the comparison between the two types of test.

Secondly, a thorough analysis of the content of the test in terms of the design specifications outlined in Chapter 2 – purpose, events, skills, functions, levels, etc – should be carried out to ensure that the tests are in fact testing what they are expected to. The more comprehensive the original design, the more fruitful will be this construct validation.

Thirdly, correlational factorial techniques can be used to indicate the factor patterns underlying test performance. Of special interest will be the underlying relationships between the first (general) and second (specific) tiers of tests, between objectively and subjectively rated performances, and between the various modes and mode combinations used. It is becoming increasingly accepted that we cannot rely on correlational techniques alone to fill in gaps in our knowledge of performance variables. They are mainly useful in indicating relationships between variables which have already been specified. Construct validation on the basis of a fully articulated model, with these provisos in mind, can therefore provide valuable insights for test development.

Fourthly, operational validation can be carried out by assessing whether, or to what extent, the decisions based on the test information are appropriate ones; whether, for example, the predictions about overall performance were realized, or whether the diagnostic findings on profile element performance were accurate.

Our conclusion to date must be that test construction is a lengthy business with much attention given to design, try-out, analysis and validation of various kinds.

Note:

We have been unable, for test security reasons, to provide actual examples of test items developed and used on a wide scale. The items quoted above have been devised to illustrate certain aspects of test development and have not been tried out.

4. Operating the test instrument

We now come to the final stage in test construction, the operation of the test instrument we have devised in prototype form. Three phases are suggested: the application of the test on a wider scale, the use of the test for practical, operational purposes and its revision in the light of its proven operational value.

Wide-scale use of the test

At a certain stage a decision has to be made about whether the test so far developed is ready for actual use. This decision is not easy, yet precise timing is essential, since there is a time beyond which trials on 'guinea-pig' testees cease to be of real value. A testee's performance is very much different when he knows, or suspects, that the test has no relevance to his future, and the enthusiasm of a teacher is similarly reduced when he knows that the test is only a 'dry run'. On the other hand, it could be premature to use as a definitive instrument a test for which items had not been analysed or for which performance norms had not been established, or which was full of misprints and faulty instructions.

For purpose-specific testing, it would be preferable to go into full operational use earlier rather than later, possibly employing an existing instrument as a back-up for a transitional period, using the track record of the past to inform the new. There are a number of reasons for this approach. First, the appropriate activities, skills and functions have been clearly specified in advance and their justification does not rest on the experimental results of tests. Again, the band method of item analysis has already built in an element of standard-setting in clearly spelt-out performance scales. The large samples needed for the standard setting and item analysis procedures of norm-referenced tests are much less necessary; indeed for such purpose-specific tests it may not be possible to obtain large numbers of trial testees or to assume that their test performances are normally distributed. The initial concurrent establishment of validity and standards via interim criteria will be the basis for the interpretation of 'L' scores and performance profiles, backed up by existing tests of a general proficiency nature, especially if these are the first element of the double-tier system described below.

Tests designed in terms of a detailed needs analysis are more ready for use than those whose construction uses an item analysis procedure primarily aimed at producing test homogeneity. Our preference, therefore, has been to move out of a pre-test context as soon as a workable testing system has been designed, to rely on the initial needs analysis rather than on large numbers of elaborate statistical manipulations, and to make test development a continuous rather than a one-off process.

The two-tier testing system

One of the problems posed in the teaching and testing of languages for specific purposes is a purely practical one: how can we possibly devise a separate test to meet every separate pattern of communicative needs? If no one pattern is equally applicable to all communicative settings, must we demand a specially-designed test for each setting? Even if such a diversified approach were desirable, it would be necessary on the grounds of feasibility and economy alone to exploit every opportunity for pooling test content.

To assist in the solution of this problem we may refer again to the *usage/use* dichotomy. Language *usage* is related to the mastery of systems which enable a user to compose correct sentences; language *use* is concerned with the extent to which a user can turn his mastery of usage to achieve a communicative purpose. It is useful also to bear in mind Widdowson's distinction between *signification*, the meaning of an utterance in grammatical terms, and *communicative value*, the meaning of an utterance when put to communicative use (Widdowson, 1978).

The ability to compose correct sentences is a crucial component of communicative performance, and this mastery is a valid area for language testing. Mastery of usage is not synonymous with mastery of use; however, for testing purposes, it may be assumed that a person who can compose correct sentences is *more likely* to be able to communicate effectively than one who cannot do so, and that a person who is unable to compose correct sentences is *less likely* to communicate effectively than one who is able to do so.

It should therefore be possible to devise a basic, wide coverage test to assess linguistic competence in terms of usage, drawing on generally-needed language skills and contexts and used as a basic 'first-tier' instrument for the establishment of comparability between groups with varying communicative needs. A test of this type does not, of course, fully cover the specific communicative needs of disparate groups of learners and must be supplemented by tests specifically designed to assess the skills and content areas needed. We refer to those specific tests as 'second-tier' tests.

Figure 14 illustrates the way in which these two tiers of tests can be integrated to create a system sensitive to the special requirements of particular learners and yet capable of providing a basis for wider comparisons. The significance of the scores on the various profile elements is heavily dependent on their stability and precision as separate measurements; if the basis of element measurement lacks precision, variations in a performance profile will reflect measurement error as much as actual performance.

In the diagram, two first-tier tests, A and B, assess the mastery of usage, and three second-tier tests, X, Y and Z, assess performance much more directly related to specific communicative tasks. The

Figure 14: Two-tier tests in bands

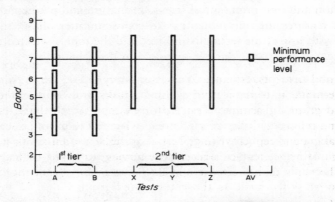

first-tier tests cover skills and functions likely to be common to a range of tasks and might be designed to assess mastery of the following:

Skill   (Munby, 1978)
Number

19. Deducing the meaning of unfamiliar lexis.
20. Understanding explicitly-stated information.
21. Understanding information not explicitly stated.
24. Understanding conceptual meanings, especially quantity, definiteness, comparison, time, location, means, cause, result, reason.
26. Understanding communicative value of an utterance with and without explicit indicators.
28. Understanding relations within a sentence, especially elements of sentence structure, negation, modals, intra-sentential connectors, embedding.
30. Understanding lexical cohesion devices: synonymy, hyponomy, antithesis, collocation, pro-forms/general words.
32. Understanding grammatical cohesion devices: anaphoric and cataphoric reference, substitution, ellipsis, time/place relaters, logical connectors.
34. Interpreting text by:
    exophoric reference, reading between lines, integration with own experience.

In some cases it might be useful to include skills related to the perception and interpretation of stress, intonation and phonemic and graphic features in continuous texts. As this first-tier phase is concerned with *usage*, the testing is indirect and the topics selected need not focus on any particular occupational or disciplinary area.

The second-tier tests, designed to assess mastery of *use*, are likely to be multiple-mode tests replicating authentic tasks and using authentic oral and graphic discourse. Test X, for example, might be a test of study and reference skills; Test Y, a read-write test requiring research, note-making and report writing; Test Z could be a listen-speak test in the form of a face-to-face structured interview followed by a group task. The skills to be tested could be taken mainly from the more operational skills, such as those numbered from 37 to 52 in the Business Studies specification (Appendix I). The tasks and topic areas should reflect as much as possible the events and activities of the specified job.

It may be possible, with large numbers, to incorporate an inter-level of tests with a broad disciplinary emphasis either on the Arts/Humanities or on the Sciences/Technologies. This would give a range of tiers: first-tier (general), middle-tier (group) and second-tier (specific) which would be applied with increasing degrees of specificity to the test groups.

The operation of test instruments

Introduction

The part testing may play in the conduct of language programmes is shown in diagrammatic form in Figure 15 (adapted from a diagram devised by Ian Seaton, British Council).

As tests are devices for assisting in making decisions about learners and programmes, whether, or to what extent, a particular type of test will be used depends on the decision to be made at that time. We shall

Figure 15: Programme – test relationship

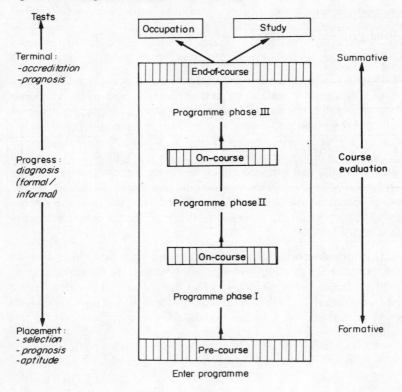

The diagram shows the three temporal testing phases:

Pre-course – {
placement,
prognosis,
aptitude.
}

On-course – {
progress, diagnosis,
course evaluation (formative).
}

End-of-course – {
accreditation,
prognosis,
course evaluation (summative).
}

examine the main test types listed above and see how they may be used in making such decisions.

Placement tests

Our experience has been mostly with two main types of placement tests; first, those assessing the linguistic suitability of applicants for training courses which demand a fair level of competence in English; secondly, those given to students with a variety of objectives who wish to enter an English language course. The purpose of the first is to decide whether the candidate's mastery of English is sufficient to allow him to benefit from a course in, say, Engineering or, if it is not, what kind of language tuition he would need to reach the required level. The purpose of the second is to assess an applicant's language level so that he can be placed in a class suitable for his abilities. In both cases, the establishing of the learner's communicative needs with the maximum degree of precision is of great value for devising the appropriate tests and programmes.

In operating the placement test, a target level profile is matched against a learner-performance profile, using the nine levels and selected profile elements illustrated in Figure 9, Chapter 3. As examples, Figure 16a, b and c show the performance profiles of three candidates for a course in Medicine at a British University, and compare their profiles with the estimated target level profile for the proposed course. The target level profile is marked T, the candidate profiles are marked A, B and C respectively.

As is typical with Medical courses, the target level to be attained is quite high, with three test elements at Band 7 and two at Band 6.

The diagrams show that Candidate A (Figure 16a) has already reached the target level profile on all of the elements, his average band score being 7.3 as against the target level average of 6.6. Candidate B (Figure 16b) with an average band score of 3.1 nowhere approaches performance at target level. Candidate C (Figure 16c) is a less clear-cut case, with an average band score of 6.2 being just below the target level profile on four of the test elements and just achieving it on one element.

T.C.P.—F

Figure 16a: ELTS individual profile sheet

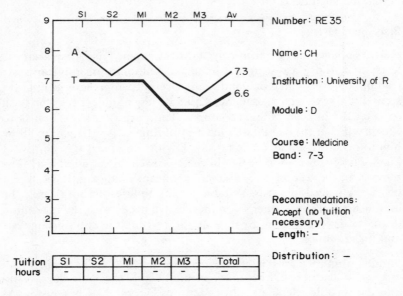

Tuition hours	SI	S2	MI	M2	M3	Total
	-	-	-	-	-	-

All three candidates are acceptable as far as their academic qualifications are concerned, but the Director of the Medical Course has now to assess their capacity to face the language demands. Candidate A will present no problem and should prove acceptable. Candidate B's performance on the language tests is so far below target level in every respect that he can safely be rejected on language grounds alone. Candidate C, whose performance profile lies just below the target level profile is a more difficult problem and several factors will have to be considered in making a decision about him.

The first is the degree of confidence we can place in the profile measurements themselves. Both the performance and the target level profiles will have an error component deriving from the fallibility of the judgements made on several elements and the inherent variability of test scores. Any estimates of test reliability or standard error will provide guidance as to the size of the error and allow us to sketch in a 'grey area' around each of the profiles being matched.

Figure 16b: Individual profile sheet

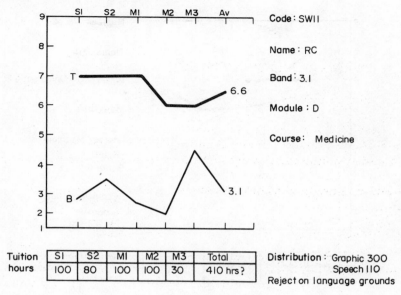

Tuition hours	SI	S2	MI	M2	M3	Total
	100	80	100	100	30	410 hrs?

Distribution : Graphic 300
Speech 110
Reject on language grounds

The second factor is the assessment of the effects of any decision taken, broadly speaking, by comparing the benefits and penalties of accepting an unsuitable candidate and rejecting a suitable one. If there are no other suitable applicants for a place, if there is a wide tolerance of language errors on the course, if the applicant is a person of great significance in the development of his own country and if he is not seriously deficient on key profile elements, he will tend to receive the benefit of the doubt and be accepted, possibly with a prescription for suitable language tuition. If, on the other hand, the pool of applicants is large, there is little tolerance for language errors, the applicant is not of key significance, his profile deficiency is in a key element, or language training is not available, then there are several excellent reasons for playing safe and rejecting, or perhaps relegating, his application.

The decision thus rests on two main areas – one basically statistical, in which is assessed the trustworthiness of the measurements of the

Figure 16c: Individual profile sheet

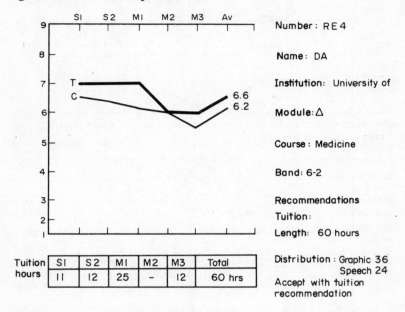

Number: RE 4

Name: DA

Institution: University of

Module: △

Course: Medicine

Band: 6-2

Recommendations
Tuition:

Length: 60 hours

Tuition hours	SI	S2	MI	M2	M3	Total
	11	12	25	–	12	60 hrs

Distribution: Graphic 36
                    Speech 24
Accept with tuition
recommendation

profile; the other basically managerial, in which are balanced the effects of alternative decisions. The task of the tester is to make the tests as accurate, relevant and explicit as possible for those who have to make such managerial decisions.

Placement decisions about language tuition are of a rather different type in that there is no one minimum acceptance profile but a series of profiles representing the various levels at which courses are conducted. Furthermore, the final target level profile is essentially the decision of the learner, and it is for him to decide whether he aims at a high level of oral proficiency, or study skills, etc. Public examinations often provide a target for those with an imprecise notion of their own language goals. A reasonably accurate assessment of initial performance levels and final target levels for groups of students, however, will allow for systematic course planning. If, for example, a language school runs four levels of course, from basic to advanced, covering a range from beginner (Band 1/0) to target level performer (say, Band 7), the placement test might place students as follows:

Course	Bands	Estimated hours to target	
Advanced	5·5 and above	max 190	min 150
Intermediate	4·5 to 5·4	max 310	min 250
Elementary	3·0 to 4·4	max 500	min 400
Basic	Below 3·0	max ?	min 500

Note: recent evidence suggests that progress at higher levels requires more tutorial time than at lower levels.

Bands	Approx. no. hrs. per band
1–2	50
2–3	70
3–4	90
4–5	100
5–6	120
6–7	250
7–8	400

As initial decisions about language course placement are not immutable, and there is usually a possibility of re-allocating students during the course, the initial placement tests need not always be very precise and could be conducted in two phases, the first focused on language usage and scored rapidly and objectively and the second task-orientated, such as a writing and interview assessment. Special attention could be reserved for borderline cases, and a review of placement could later be made on the basis of further, on-course testing supplemented by teacher rating.

Prognostic tests

If it is difficult to assess accurately a person's present level of performance, it is well nigh impossible to make a precise prediction of his future performance. The record of prognostic tests, including those classified as 'aptitude' tests, is not impressive. The content of such tests includes discrimination of sounds, matching of words, learning of elements of strange invented languages and recording of the testees' attitudes, interests and linguistic history. The criteria of aptitude include assessments of the comparative ease and rapidity of later effective learning.

However, the efficiency of such prognostications, in correlation terms, is low. The correlations, in the order of 0.4 and 0.5, represent a forecasting efficiency of about 10% better than chance, but there is no inherent reason why prognostic measures should not be considerably improved.

The source of such improvement would lie in a greater specificity of the criteria against which prognosis could be judged, a greater range of attitudes and behaviours to be incorporated in the initial and final tests, an improvement in the accuracy and delicacy of measurements of linguistic behaviour, and measures to partial out the effects of irrelevant factors on the learning. In other words, very great specificity must replace the vagueness of such terms as 'language aptitude'. Until this is done, the results of individual aptitude tests are hardly likely to justify the time and resources expended on them. However, reasonable forecasts can be made of *group* progress on the basis of recorded trends.

Progress tests

The essence of progress testing is to measure to what extent learning goals are being achieved. In the instruments already described, progress means filling the gap between an individual's initial performance profile and the target level profile appropriate to his needs. The test used for measuring progress should derive from the initial needs analysis and be presented in similar format. In interpreting results, account should be taken of error and reliability factors and the search for causes of progress or lack of it should involve scrutiny not only of the learner but also of the programme he is following.

Observational, or non-interactional, measurement techniques and self-assessment ratings can be valuable adjuncts to the more formal and conventional methods of assessing progress.

Diagnostic tests

Diagnostic tests are closely related to progress tests, but their emphasis is on a closer study of specific elements of performance to establish the causes lying behind learning progress – or lack of it – so that remedial action can be taken. Any test results which can be presented in profile form have diagnostic potential. For example, the three candidate profiles in Figure 16 above show the strengths and weaknesses of the three individuals and relate their performances to the demands indicated in the target level profile. However, the diagnosis so made is comparatively coarse, and effective remedial action requires a more delicate picture of the reasons behind particular performance deficiencies. For this purpose the taxonomy of language skills shown in Appendix I may be profitably used, uncovering enabling-skill deficiencies which might contribute towards defective performance in use-based tasks.

For example, a student may not handle effectively certain transcoding tasks involving the interpretation of diagrams in written language. The problem may be rooted either in his lack of mastery of diagram conventions or in the inadequacy of his language skills, or in both. The learner's knowledge of diagram conventions can then be examined – does he understand the relationship between two axes of a graphic presentation, the trend expressed by a curve and the relationships expressed with two or more curves? The linguistic patterns may also be examined – does he understand the language terms for describing dimensions and trends, for comparing and contrasting and for expressing causality? Or perhaps he suffers from a combination of language and representational deficiencies which would point to a sizeable programme of improvement in both subject and language skills.

In the second example of diagnosis, the sub-skills needed for satisfactory handling of a higher level skill are identified in order to track down the basic causes of a communication problem. We list below some of the sub-skills which could contribute to the operation of skill number 40.3: *Extracting salient points to summarize the underlying idea of a test.*

Contributing skills might be:

39.1/6 Distinguishing main idea by differentiation between details of primary and secondary significance, and fact from opinion.

35.5   Recognizing indicators in discourse for emphasizing a point.

32.6   Understanding text relations through the grammatical cohesion device of logical connection.

30.6/7 Understanding text relations through lexical cohesion devices of collocation and pro-forms.

24.7   Understanding conceptual meaning especially cause, result and reason.

19.2   Deducing the meaning of unfamiliar words through contextual clues.

17.1/3 Recognizing the script by distinguishing graphemes and understanding punctuation.

Diagnosis of spoken text problems may involve probing phonic features such as the perception and interpretation of phonemes, or stress and intonation in connected speech. The word diagnosis is here used in the medical sense, that is, the search for the contributory causes of a malfunction, in this instance, impediments to communication. Insofar as the inventory of language skills is hierarchical, or taxonomic, the causes of a higher level malfunction will tend to be traced back through the inventory, as exemplified in the example above.

Diagnosis may be carried out by checking through the different levels of performance in terms of the performance criteria elaborated in Appendix III. If a testee is unable to cope with material of target level size, complexity, range and speed, he may be presented with materials at intermediate or basic level to discover which text features are presenting special difficulty. As one of the most common causes of learning problems is the use of texts which are too difficult, an examination of the features of text difficulty may suggest that the learning problem lies in certain text characteristics. The solution can then be either to use more suitable texts or to improve the learner's text-handling skills.

In diagnostic testing, then, we can draw extensively on the prior specification of language skills; the more detailed and accurate the specification, the more effective should be the diagnosis.

Accreditation tests

Alongside the test types we have been considering are public examinations, conducted at regular intervals by established bodies and offering the means of obtaining widely-recognized certificates attesting to levels of language proficiency.

The formal and public character of the examinations gives a wide currency to their results, so that people can assess competence by reference to an established certificate of known value. However, this broad universality may be purchased at the expense of individual requirements which are only partially met by the examination.

Because they are designed to establish and maintain standards, the content and format of the examination tend to be inflexible; any change, particularly if it involves testing at lower levels, may be seen as a threat to such standards. Even an acknowledged improvement may be resisted because it will disturb the basis for comparable standards. Change can also be seen as a breach of faith with learners aspiring to enter the examination in the future.

The wide territorial coverage of the public examination also means that it has to reject content likely to be of relevance only to individuals or small groups. The commonality of usage-based tests and their ease of administration makes them a favourite, whereas use-based tests, drawing on authentic texts and contexts, are much more troublesome to devise, apply and assess. The introduction of mixed mode testing and ESP modules thus becomes an irritating complication.

Despite their influence on curricula and teaching methods, examinations rarely aim to present a fully spelt-out rationale describing the language needs to be met or the syllabus content and the suggested learning sequences to be followed.

Finally, because of all the above constraining circumstances, there must be a strong emphasis on security; the authenticity, interaction, reference to sources of information and spontaneous behaviour essential to communication may well be drained from the examination setting.

None of the above dilemmas are easy to resolve because the constraints of efficient tests and examinations and the requirements of genuine linguistic communication are in conflict with each other.

Examinations have a part to play in reinforcing the curriculum triangle, but they defeat this purpose when they dictate the nature of programmes, pre-empt the fulfilment of genuine needs and become objectives in their own right. To reconcile these demands is difficult but necessary if public examinations are to retain their credibility.

Programme evaluation and management

The judgement of the success or otherwise of a language programme is not wholly a quantifiable business. Many of the relevant questions can be answered by the considered, but subjective, opinions of experienced observers. These opinions can be supported by factual statements, again expressed verbally. But no programme evaluation can be considered complete without the presentation of some quantitative data about the progress of the course participants.

Certain kinds of information provided by test data will assist in making informed decisions about programmes. The first, shown in Figure 17, illustrates the progress of a group of students in a 300 hour language programme.

The purpose of compiling this chart was to make a broad assessment of students' progress during their language training. Three sets of tests were given, Test I on arrival, Test II after 200 hours of tuition, and Test III after a further 100 hours of tuition. The distribution of student scores on each testing occasion is clearly shown by the chart. On arrival, the groups represented a wide range of language performance, ranging from Band 2 to Band 7. On the second and third occasions, the distributions of performance do not shift as a block to the right

Figure 17: Student group progress chart

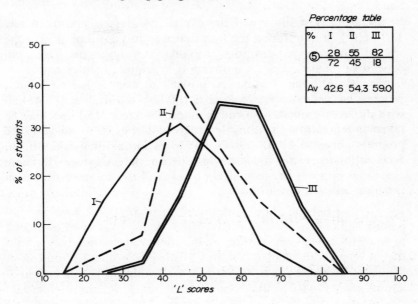

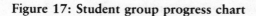

but, as it were, tilt on a comparatively stable base, indicating that students do not learn at a common rate, and that some may learn very little. In any group there may be not only a wide spread of language proficiency but also differences in rates of progress during tuition. It is possible to examine progress by finding the percentage of students who reach particular band levels. The percentage table in Figure 17, for example, gives the proportion of students above and below Band 5.0 on the three test occasions. It can be seen that the initial proportions (28:72) are reversed at the final occasion (82:18). If final and intermediate targets are set, say, at Band 6.0 and 4.0 respectively, we can estimate how many students reach either target. If, for example, 6.5 had been the target, this particular course could not be judged to have been particularly successful as only approximately 30% of students achieved that level.

Perhaps the most generally useful statistic for assessing progress is the average number of hours it takes a student to progress by one band.

In the group just illustrated the overall progress is approximately 190 hpb, 170 hpb during the first semester and 210 hpb during the second. The expected progress, as expressed in hours per band, will depend on factors such as motivation, teaching facilities and sheer hard work. Although it is not yet possible to work in precise figures, progress has been observed as fast as 100 hpb and as slow as 300 hpb with different groups. As a rough guide, therefore, 150 hpb may be taken as representing reasonable progress. The evidence suggests the progress curve to be an ogive, that is an initial slow take-off, an acceleration thereafter and a slowing down at the final stage. (But note again that progress between higher bands will require more time than progress between lower bands.)

The hours-per-band (hpb) index can be of practical assistance in predicting language tuition needs. From Figure 16, can be estimated for students B and C the nature and duration of the tuition they should require to meet the demands shown by the job profile. For student B, assuming 25 hours per band per test, we would propose a course of approximately 410 contact hours, or about 4 months of full-time tuition, with a heavy emphasis on graphic skills. For student C, we would propose a course of 60 contact hours, or about two weeks of full-time tuition, with some emphasis on oral skills. We must again stress that a good deal of work still needs to be done on refining the bases of these calculations, but the broad principles and their operational value seem clear.

Yet another application of data to course operation can be seen in Figure 18 in which, using data from earlier courses, an estimate can be made of the numbers of students likely to reach given target levels at various stages during a course.

Estimates of percentages expected to reach given targets:

Band	200hrs	400hrs	600hrs
5.0	30	58	73
6.0	20	43	60
6.5	10	28	48

Figure 18: Prediction of progress

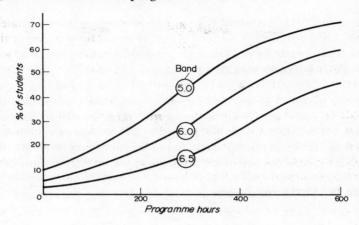

Certain assumptions have to be made in interpreting these curves, namely, that past groups are broadly similar in character to the one being examined and that conditions of learning and teaching are roughly the same, and these assumptions can be checked in due course. We thus have a device which will allow prediction of the percentages of students still likely to require tuition after given stages in the life of a course – obviously an important factor in making financial, staff and accommodation arrangements. Although more work is needed to perfect this prediction system, this sort of procedure is better than the common assumption that all students, whatever their proficiency, should require the same duration of programme.

Among the many other possible uses of programme feedback, there is the possibility of comparing the progress of different groups of students or of several individual students and also of examining current teaching issues. At present, for example, there is much controversy about the relative emphasis to be put on teaching communication (or *use*) skills as against teaching code (or *usage*) skills. A fair assessment could not be made with *usage* tests alone, or with *use* tests alone, but would require some form of two-tier test instrument. Such issues are much more amenable to meaningful discussion if we can devise and use accurate test instruments in their solution.

Revision of test systems

However useful the tests may be, they cannot be excused rigorous scrutiny to see if it is possible to improve them as aids to decision-making. Their relevance can be checked by a thorough examination to see if they are in fact testing the skills and functions originally specified and that they are not beginning to focus simply on testing those areas

Figure 19: Model for programme/test development and revision

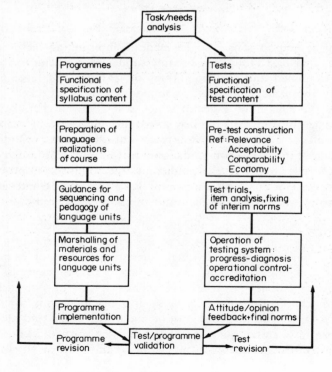

which are easy to test. They can also be operationally validated to discover how far the decisions about placement, prognosis, diagnosis, progress and accreditation accord with subsequent performance.

Performance must also be related to that in other comparable tests and to independent criteria, in order to assess their congruence with the theoretical model behind their design; all these factors can be constantly checked.

These prolonged processes of test and programme development might be thought to ensure the production of definitive instruments. Unfortunately, such is not the case: no sooner have instruments been produced than they have to be re-examined for relevance, acceptability, comparability and economy and the whole process to be gone through again so that, however asymptotically, we gradually approach the production of the best possible test system.

The model shown in Figure 19 illustrates the continuity of the processes of test design, development, operation and revision.

5. Communicative testing literature

Introduction

It is unfortunate that the adventurous thinking taking place in the field of applied linguistics, communication and socio-linguistics is not being matched in the field of testing.

We need a model sufficiently comprehensive to subsume relevant features of social behaviour, of discourse and language, and sufficiently detailed to indicate which language skills, functions and patterns should be tested, and within which contexts. The following quotations summarize current thinking on communicative language study and the implications for testing. In some of these quotations, small – and insignificant – alterations have been made in the text for ease of reading. Full references are given in the bibliography.

1. K E Morrow: *Techniques of evaluation for a notional syllabus*

The use of language in a communicative situation has a number of features which are not measured in conventional language tests. In the overwhelming majority of cases language in use is based on an interaction. An important feature of the interaction is its unpredictability. Any use of language will take place in a clearly defined and delimited context. Authentic language, with rare exceptions, is not simplified to take account of the linguistics abilities of the addressee.

2. K E Morrow: *Communicative language testing: revolution or evolution?*

One of the characteristic features of the communicative approach to language teaching is that it obliges us (or enables us) to make assumptions about the types of communication we will equip learners to handle. This applies equally to communicative testing. This means that there is unlikely to be, in communicative terms, a single overall test of language proficiency. What will be offered are tests of proficiency (at different levels) in terms of specified communicative criteria. First the concept of pass: fail loses much of its force; every candidate can be assessed in terms of what he can do. Secondly, language performance can be differentially assessed in different communicative areas. The third implication is perhaps the most far-reaching. The importance of specifying the communicative criteria in terms of which assessment is being offered, means that examining bodies will have to draw up, and probably publish, specifications of the types of operation they intend to test, the content areas to which they will relate and the criteria which will be adopted in assessment.

3. J A van Ek: *The threshold level in a unit/credit system*

Language is a means of communication. The aim of foreign language learning is first and foremost the ability to communicate verbally. Language learning objectives, therefore, are to be defined in terms of 'adequate verbal behaviour in language communication situations.'

4. L G Alexander: *Waystage and threshold level: some methodological implications*

Waystage and threshold level specifications can be manipulated to yield criteria for testing. Ideally, testing objectives should be the same as teaching objectives, so there is no conflict between the two activities. It is possible that entirely new kinds of tests will have to be developed to accompany functionally-based courses, for we are ultimately concerned not with how much the student knows, but how well he performs.

5. D A Wilkins: *The general structure of a unit/credit system for adult language learning*

The unit/credit system requires that one should know who the differing categories of learners are and what their linguistic needs are likely to be. Research ... has provided a set of communicative categories in terms of which individual language needs can be predicted and specific language syllabuses developed.

6. Eugene J Brière: *Are we really measuring proficiency with our foreign language tests?*

Spolsky points out that the layman's criterion for knowing a language is usually expressed in some type of functional statement. For example, 'He knows enough French to read a newspaper and ask simple questions for directions.' Statements such as these refer to language *use* and not to grammar or phonology. The question then arises, how does one go about deciding when someone knows enough language to carry out a specific function? One approach would be to give someone a language-using test to perform, such as having a physics major listen to a lecture on thermodynamics and then test the comprehension.

7. P M Rea: *Assessing language as communication*

The important point which emerges is that the emphasis is on a person's ability to communicate with ease and effect in specified sociolinguistic settings.

Following on from this, any test should, desirably, be capable of defining the extent to which a person can or cannot operate in the target language, a test should seek therefore to provide useful and diagnostic information.

'Communicative' language tests for personal and professional purposes imply a set of testing 'tasks' which reflect and simulate actual linguistic demands within specified domains. The emphasis is on the communicative behaviour of people, on the speech acts that occur and the interactive relationships that link speech acts to form coherent discourse.

Our tests are indeed valid if our test design is a true reflection and measure of communicative language performance within a specified domain.

8. J A Upshur: *Measurement of oral communication*

Jakobovits (1968) has shown the theoretical inadequacies of 'pattern practice' learning, and Brière (1968) has documented the 'patternese' responses (not necessarily indicative of speaking ability) to 'pattern-practice' testing. Spolsky has consistently argued the limitations of judgements based on language-like behaviour (such as dialogue recitations) and the need for tests of 'creative use' of language.

9. B. Spolsky *et al: Functional tests of oral proficiency*

It is clear that levels of knowing a language cannot be characterized in specific linguistic terms, that is, as mastery of criterion percentage of items in a grammar and lexicon. Proficiency tests must be based on a functional definition of levels. Tests are needed not of how many items a subject may know (although, of course, this is a reasonable question in an achievement or diagnostic test) but of his ability to operate in a specified sociolinguistic situation with ease and effect.

10. I F Roos–Wijgh, from Clark (ed): *Direct testing of speaking proficiency*

'Testing speaking proficiency through functional dialogues'

We hope that the use of these tests will contribute to new developments . . . students will then be motivated, because they will find that they can really 'do something' with the language. What they have learned at school will enable them to make contact with foreigners and to communicate with them.

11. J L Munby: *Communicative syllabus design*

This book is an attempt to solve this problem by designing a dynamic processing model that starts with the learner and ends with his target communicative competence. It is the detailed syllabus specification, the target communicative competence, which constitutes the essence of what should be embodied in the course materials. The model does not deal with materials production and so no more than an indication is given of the implementational constraints on the syllabus specification, eg the number of trained teachers available, quantity of instruction, the expectations of the institution, traditional strategies of learning, etc. It is pointed out that such variables, although important in the modification of syllabus specifications and the production/selection of materials, belong to the subsequent stage of course design and should not be considered before the syllabus specification has been obtained.

12. Ibid

It seems clear that communicative competence includes the ability to use linguistic forms to perform communicative acts and to understand the communicative functions of sentences and their relationships to other sentences. This happens at the level of discourse and involves, *inter alia*, knowledge of the rhetorical rules of use that govern the patterning of such acts, the interpretative strategies of the language user (Widdowson, 1975), and also what Candlin (1976) has described as the contextual meaning of an utterance (the value derived from its positional significance in the discourse). These discourse units (rhetorical acts, speech functions) have characteristics and formal rules of occurrence that can be and need to be made explicit. More analyses and descriptions are needed, such as those provided by Sinclair *et al* (1972), Candlin *et al* (1974) and, on a smaller scale, Ervin–Tripp (1972).

The implications for the model include the following:

1. Selecting communicative units, such as speech functions or rhetorical acts, rather than grammatical elements in the specification of a syllabus, takes place at the level of discourse.
2. Theoretical rules and contextual meaning are as important as grammatical rules and referential meaning, so they should be taught as appropriate to the required acts and functions.
3. A concern with communicative competence indicates the need for redefining the dimensions of syllabus specifications to take account of the communicative value of discourse level units.

13. Ibid

Jakobovits makes some important points about the relation of communicative competence to language testing. In discussing the inadequacy of the discrete-point approach (still the major one today) to language testing and teaching, he points out that experience has shown that 'performance on these language tests and the ability to make use of the language for communicative purposes are not necessarily related, indicating that the former is not a good measure of the latter'. In view of the importance of the latter, and the current lack of a clear and comprehensive answer to the question of what it is to know how to use a language, he suggests the pragmatic strategy of making detailed definitions of 'specific communicative goals and of assessing the extent to which an individual is capable of meeting these goals'. He also recognizes that there are different levels of communicative competence and, like Hymes, allows for less than native language competence in the specification that should be made of the different levels of proficiency that are relevant to a second language learner.

14. D K Stevenson: *Beyond faith and face validity*

There is a great tendency to rush to measurement, to gather data first, and hypothesise later.

15. J A Fishman and **R L Cooper:** *The socio-linguistic foundations of language testing*

A socio-linguistic approach to the construction of language assessment procedures . . . insists upon the specification of the communicative contexts in which the behaviour to be assessed occurs and can be justified on two grounds. First, language behaviour . . . varies as a function of context . . . Second, language assessment procedures have been successfully contextualized so as to gather data reflecting systematic socio-linguistic variation.

Authors of language assessment procedures, therefore, should consider the context in which the behaviours they wish to describe take place. The more the criterion behaviour varies as a function of context, the more important it is to construct techniques which can reflect variation.

*   *   *   *

The above reflect many of the main points of our theme, not least that the testing of a knowledge of language patterns is only part of the story of communicative performance testing. (I am grateful to Ian Seaton for suggesting some of the quotations.)

Some experimental data

During 1975 and 1976, a group of 160 overseas students came to

Britain to undergo a basic course of combined Science and English and were given a series of tests of their competence in English. The group showed a good deal of progress on the tests used, averaging about Band 3 on arrival and reaching well into Band 6 at the end of the nine-month academic year. The three main test phases took place soon after arrival, about the middle of the course, and towards the end of the course. The full test battery consisted of eight tests, and the tutors also gave class grades in Science subjects, and English language grades based on their knowledge of the students' day-to-day work. Quite elaborate statistical analyses – including variance, factor and principle component analyses – were carried out on the resultant data, and we will present below some of the results in order to show that extended measurement and elaborate data handling may prove curiously unrewarding.

Figure 20 shows the intercorrelations between the various test scores of the final testing. The actual tests given were:

1   *Comprehension,* a test of the students' sensitivity to short texts in English, so framed as to evoke judgements and attitudes as well as factual information.
2   *Essay,* the writing of two short essays, one on a scientific topic, the other on a more general topic.
3/4 *Cloze,* a moderately simple piece of scientific writing with every tenth word omitted. The responses were marked twice, once recognizing any 'acceptable' response, and once recognizing only the 'exact' word in the original text.
5   *Structure,* a discrete-item test of English structure, vocabulary and usage with a focus on scientific usage.
6   *Dictation,* a dictation passage, with one mark awarded for each word recognizably written down.
7/8 *Spanish Cloze,* a piece of writing similar in type to that of the English cloze test, but in Spanish (the students' native language), to be answered in Spanish. The responses were marked, as with the English cloze, both as 'acceptable' and 'exact'.
9   *Class Grade,* tutors' general impression of the students' competence in Science and general subjects.
10   *Language Grade,* an assessment of students' competence to

follow their course in English, given by tutors familiar with each student.

Figure 20: Correlation matrix of English scores of 156 students in final test battery (Decimal points omitted)

Variable	1 Compreh	2 Essay	3 Cl (ac)	4 Cl (ex)	5 Struct	6 Dict	7 Sp (ac)	8 Sp (ex)
1 Comprehension	–	355	461	431	472	422	424	430
2 Essay	355	–	529	480	430	584	270	302
3 Cloze (ac)	461	529	–	899	623	621	468	447
4 Cloze (ex)	431	480	899	–	587	614	455	423
5 Structure	472	430	623	587	–	590	468	486
6 Dictation	422	584	621	614	590	–	421	426
7 Spanish (ac)	424	270	468	455	468	421	–	931
8 Spanish (ex)	430	302	447	423	486	426	931	–
9 Class grade	365	415	358	360	315	464	368	417
10 Language grade	351	496	538	535	446	574	330	355

(r 9:10 = 0·468)

We can see from Figure 20 that the inter-test correlations are only moderate in size, from about 0.3 to a little over 0.6, except for those between the cloze 'acceptable' and 'exact' which reach 0.899 for the English cloze and 0.931 for the Spanish cloze. These high correlations are in fact spurious in that there is considerable content overlap between the 'acceptable' and the 'exact' versions. Otherwise, inspection of the correlation matrix reveals very little of behavioural significance. We see relatively high correlations between cloze, structure and dictation, and relatively low ones between Spanish cloze and essay. Comprehension seems to occupy a space in the middle-sized range of correlations.

We will look at the correlation patterns shortly, but can note now one very significant point – we do not really know the precise behaviour which lies behind the various test labels. The behaviour elicited in, for example, the essay test is different from that elicited in the structure test, the former being completely productive, the latter being of recognition of acceptable alternatives. Dictation, with an element of listening and interpretation of spoken utterances, is clearly different from both essay and structure. But where are the real differences and overlaps? Again, in relating the various tests to class grades, we see that class grade has a relatively high correlation with Spanish 'exact', although little use is made of Spanish, at least overtly, as the course proceeds.

In Figure 21 we show a principal component analysis of the matrix given in Figure 20. The analysis given in Figure 21 indicates four

Figure 21: Principle component analysis of correlation matrix, Figure 20 (above)

Variables	Components			
	I	*II*	*III*	*IV*
1 Comprehension	252	082	163	153
2 Essay	292	−340	−449	−146
3 Cloze (acceptable)	414	−183	332	−589
4 Cloze (exact)	278	−123	216	−397
5 Structure	424	−047	560	579
6 Dictation	474	−348	−482	325
7 Spanish (acc)	326	622	−180	−100
8 Spanish (ex)	302	565	−191	−028
Percentage of variance:	58·0%	14·1%	7·9%	6·8%

Note: Coefficients of principal components in columns. The sum of squares equals unity for each component. Decimal points omitted.

components, with Component I accounting for 58.0% of the trace total variance and Component IV with only 6.8% of the variance. We can call the first component a 'general language factor' with positive loadings from all the variables and the highest loadings on dictation, structure and cloze (acceptable). Factor II is clearly identified with 'L1 performance' with high loadings in Spanish cloze (acceptable and exact), and contrastive negative loadings in dictation and essay. This factor seems to differentiate between L1 and L2 performance. Factor III, with a high loading in structure and fair loading in cloze (acceptable) and contrasting with essay and dictation could suggest an element of 'formal language pattern mastery at sentence and inter-sentential level'. Factor IV, again with a high loading in structure, a fair loading in dictation, and contrasting with cloze, could possibly be related to 'mastery of small-span intra-sentential skills' and formal correctness.

In summary, then, we could make an attempt to state the relationships between the variables in terms of these factors:

Factor I: *General communicative competence factor:*
             58.0% of variance, with positive loadings on dictation and cloze.

Factor II: *Distinctive L1 performance factor:*
             14.1% of variance, with positive loadings on Spanish tests; negative on essay and dictation.

Factor III: *Text-handling factor:*
             7.9% of variance, with positive loadings on structure and cloze; negative on essay and dictation.

Factor IV: *Intra-sentence pattern mastery factor:*
             6.8% of variance; with positive loadings on structure and dictation; negative on cloze.

Those interested in further statistical manipulations may refer to the complete table of correlations of the three test occasions in Appendix IV, page 140, and their unrotated principal component analyses. (We also have on record the loadings of the variables after varimax rotation). The data could be studied as an interesting exercise in component analysis interpretation, but we will shortcut the process by putting together, in Figure 22, the rankings of the eight variables in the four components of the three occasions.

Figure 22 shows relative loadings for all three occasions, from which we can note two particular features; first, the very stable role of dictation (111, 888, etc), secondly, the marked upward trend of structure (522, 654 etc) and the downward trend of comprehension (258, 123, etc). We can hazard a few conclusions; that dictation seemed to be a significant and stable test; that performance on the structure test gained greater significance as learning took place; that an L1 test gives information of relevance to the assessment of L2 performance. We have, however, found no justification for saying that a discrete point test (eg structure) lacks value as compared with the integrative tests (eg essay, comprehension).

On the whole, however, our conclusions are vague and uncertain and, because of the *ad hoc*, unspecific, decontextualized character of the original model and the vagueness of the labels denoting tests, we can only add piecemeal to our insights into language-learning behaviour. We feel that, even if we can now make crude decisions about the individuals or groups of learners, the whole process, in spite of the elaborate facade of test procedures and data analysis, is pre-scientific.

Figure 22: Rank order of component loadings of three analyses a, b and c (Ranks 1–8)

	Components			
Variable	*I* *a b c*	*II* *a b c*	*III* *a b c*	*IV* *a b c*
1 Comprehension	258	123	424	113
2 Essay	436	717	557	876
3 Cloze (ac)	343	476	142	648
4 Cloze (ex)	667	565	233	537
5 Structure	522	654	311	781
6 Dictation	111	888	668	222
7 Spanish (ac)	874	231	885	465
8 Spanish (ex)	785	342	776	354

(ac): acceptable; *(ex)*: exact.

Our work forces us to the conclusion that to know precisely what we are testing we will have to work within the framework of a contextualized, purposive model of adequate scope, cohesion and delicacy. We hope that, by adopting the procedures described elsewhere in the book, we are at least moving in the direction of this goal.

Measurement criteria

Because of the importance of criteria in test measurement, we will now return to a more detailed discussion of the two approaches of norm-referencing and criterion-referencing. A major difference between the two approaches rests in the distance between test and criterion, and we will attempt to illustrate this difference by an example.

Let us suppose that a military commander has to blow up an enemy post which is protected by a twelve-foot ditch. He has to select a team of men who, in attacking the post, must be able to jump the required distance in battle conditions, so he sets up a test to model as far as possible the conditions of the jump, selecting for his team those men able to jump the required distance under the given circumstances. The task is a clear, unambiguous one, the test is an accurate reflection of the task, and the criterion of selection is the answer to a simple yes-no question.

However, in measuring human behaviour, especially in its more complex fields such as language, the issues are not so clear-cut, and the classical measurement framework has been to assess performance not by direct reference to the criterion (as above) but by a comparison of the performance of an individual with that of others on the same measure, expressing his competence in terms of group norms and predicting the likelihood of his success in a task according to probability tables.

There is no inherent superiority of one approach over the other, and everything will depend on the purpose of the testing and on the accessibility of the criterion. If we wish to select the 'best' members of a group, and if the criteria are varied, complex and difficult to define, then we will no doubt use a norm-referenced approach and express our conclusions in terms of probabilities and group norms. If we wish to make a decision on a yes-no basis, to select those with an operationally-defined competence, and if the criterion is clear and accessible, then our approach will be criterion-referenced and our conclusions expressed in an appropriately simple description of behaviour.

Certain curricular areas, such as Mathematics, Science and Sports, are more amenable to criterion-referenced approaches than others. Here the tasks, experiments and calculations can be clearly specified and the results can be judged more easily as regards success and failure. In language teaching, however, the targets and criteria have been so nebulous and indeterminate that performance has had to be assessed in terms of norms. We have not been able to identify one task, or even constellation of tasks, to represent an adequate level of performance for a particular communicative purpose. What we are aiming to do in language testing, by contextualizing the tests, by carefully specifying needs and by matching up as closely as possible the test procedures and the criterion behaviour, is to move towards the direct relationship between test and criterion which is the essence of the criterion-referenced approach.

We have gone into the above distinction in some detail for a very practical purpose, which is to allow discussion about criterion-referenced tests to be based on the appropriate premises. The information about norm-referenced testing is so readily available that it is difficult not to apply norm-based criteria indiscriminately to different types of tests. Here are examples of statements rooted in a norm-based approach which do not necessarily apply to other approaches:

- this test is good, it spreads the students out nicely;
- this test is much too hard because my students couldn't do it;
- this item is too easy, we'll have to eliminate it or make the distractors more plausible;
- this student should have no problems, his score is one standard deviation above the mean;
- the test was useless, all the students passed.

Understandable in the context of one approach to measurement, such comments can be meaningless when applied to another approach. In judging the efficiency of a criterion-referenced approach, in short, the criteria of goodness applicable to a norm-referenced test are usually not only irrelevant but even harmful to test construction. The paper by Popham and Husek (1969) is a valuable reference to the above topic. We can aptly conclude the present section with some quotations from that paper:

'The problem is not only how to summarize a student's performance on a test but also how to ensure that a test is constructed, and judged, in a manner appropriate to its use, even if its use is not in the classical framework' (page 1).

'We have all read about test construction and item analysis. The procedures may not always be simple, the formulae may not be trivial; but there are hundreds of books and thousands of articles to guide us. Unfortunately, most of what these helpmates outline as 'good' things to do are not only irrelevant to criterion-referenced tests, but are actually injurious to their proper development and use. This is true because the treatment of validity, the suggestions about reliability and the formulae for item analysis are all based on the desirability of variability among scores' (page 3).

'When a writer constructs items for a norm-referenced test, he wants variability and makes all sorts of concessions to promote variant scores. He disdains items which are 'too easy' or 'too hard'. He tries to increase the allure of wrong answer options ... The criterion-referenced item writer is guided by another goal. *His chief rule is to make sure the item is an accurate reflection of the criterion behaviour*' (page 4).

'If a criterion-referenced test has a high average inter-item correlation, this is fine. If the test has a high test-retest correlation, that is also fine ... The point is that a criterion-referenced test could be highly consistent, either internally or temporarily, and yet indices dependent on variability might not reflect that consistency ... A carefully made judgment, based on the test's apparent relevance to the behaviours legitimately inferable from those delimited by the criterion, is the general procedure for validating criterion-referenced measures' (page 5).

'For criterion-referenced tests, the use of discrimination indices must be modified. An item which does not discriminate need not be eliminated. If it reflects an important attribute of the criterion, such an item should remain in the test ... Discrimination indices are little more than warning flags ... (indeed) should criterion-referenced measures be subject to item analysis operations?' (page 6).

Conclusion

I believe that in the preceding chapters I have been able to establish both a case for profound unease about the bases of much current language testing and a rationale for the development of principles and procedures by which we can align our measurement systems more closely with the operational role they are required to play. What I have described in this book is part of a transition phase from the language-based design approach with a classical, norm-based, approach to data handling, to a communicatively-oriented design with a criterion-oriented analysis system. In our final section we turn our attention to what might happen in the future in the development of communicative testing.

Future lines of development

In following up the suggestions put forward in this book, I divide the field into eight main topics, as follows:

1. The relationship between testing and the learning of languages: this topic includes a consideration of feedback systems of all kinds and there is every reason why native-language learning and the multiple learning of modern languages, as well as the learning of a single target language for use (eg EFL) should be a legitimate part of this research field.
2. The involvement of the learner himself through self-assessment, his interpretation of test data about himself, and his self-monitoring in learning programmes.
3. The contribution of banding systems and the improvement of their specificity and relevance, with particular emphasis on communicative activities as opposed to the conventional 'four skills'.

4. The comparability of the various test systems already widely in use; the devising of an international 'yardstick' on the basis of which the characteristics and levels of existing tests might be calibrated.

5. The exploration of different approaches to initial test design. The model which we have adopted has been carefully worked out and certainly meets many of our basic design requirements, but it is certainly not the final answer and, indeed, has as yet little empirical support in terms of scientifically collected and analysed data.

6. The 'demythologising' of language testing; as we have shown, the elaborate facade of impressive statistics can so easily cover a wholly unsatisfactory testing edifice. The basic design factors must be specific and intelligible in their own terms and there is no reason why a teacher or a learner should not be able to appreciate their main features.

7. The improved delineation of performance criteria, a potentially valuable link between the undoubtedly fruitful subjective judgements of an informed assessor and the objectivity of multiple-choice test types.

8. A number of technical questions: the relative contributions of the two levels of 'two-tier' tests with different learners and in different operational contexts, the coverage of purpose-specific modules, the optimum specificity of job-derived tests and the clarification of such traits as 'aptitude'.

Certain projects currently being worked on will provide more and more hard information on such topics and it is believed that future publications will be able to present more rounded, more authoritative, information on the principles and practice of communicative performance testing than we have done in this interim study.

Appendix I. Communication needs profile

English for Business Studies
(prepared by Roger Hawkey, slightly adapted)

Prologue: Details of participant under specification

Name:	'Audu Suleiman'
Age:	22
Primary school:	Kualle PS, Kano, Nigeria
Secondary school:	GSS, Kano
Further education:	College of Advanced Studies, Kano (1 year only)
Projected occupation:	Into father's building company as Managing Accountant
Projected UK training:	HND in Business Studies, Kingston Polytechnic

Communication needs profile

0. Participant

Identity

Age: 22
Sex: Male
Nationality: Nigerian
Place of Residence: Kano

Language

Mother tongue: Hausa
Target Language: English
Present level/command of target language: upper intermediate
Other languages known: French
Extent of command: lower intermediate

1. Purposive domain

ESP classification

English required for discipline-based, in-study educational purposes.

Educational purposes

Specific discipline: Business Studies
Central areas of study: Economics; Legal Studies; Business Accounts;
                    Statistics
Other areas of study: Marketing; Purchasing
Academic discipline classification: Social Science

2. Setting

Physical setting: spatial

Location
Country: England
Town: Kingston

Place of study and study setting
Polytechnic
Lecture room/theatre
Classroom
Seminar/tutorial
Private study/library

Other places

Industrial visit locations eg factories
Commercial visit locations eg businesses

Extent: size of institution: fairly small/fairly large

Extent: scale of use: international

Physical setting: temporal

Point of time: at all times of formal and private study; on industrial
and commercial visits

Duration: for approximately ten hours a day

Frequency: regularly during term time and, probably, during vaca-
tions

Psychosocial setting

Culturally different
Age/sex non-discriminating
Ethical
Fairly political
Quasi-professional
Educationally developed
Technologically sophisticated
Unfamiliar human
Demanding
Fairly hurried
Informal
Egalitarian
Argumentative but harmonious

3. Interaction

Position

Student

Role-set

Lecturers, teachers, tutors
Fellow students
Official contacts on industrial and commercial visits
Writers of books, papers, articles, hand-outs

Role-set identity

Number: individual/small group
Age-group: adult
Sex: mixed
Nationality: mainly British
               narrow majority British; remainder mixed
               mainly British
               mainly British or American

Social relationships

Learner to instructor/authority
Outsider to insider
Non-professional to professional
Non-native to native
Insider to insider
Adult to adult

4. Instrumentality

Medium

Spoken receptive   spoken productive
Written receptive   written productive

Mode

Monologue, spoken to be heard
Monologue, written to be read
Dialogue, spoken to be heard
Dialogue, written to be read

Channel

Face-to-face [bilateral]
Print [bilateral]
Face-to-face [unilateral]
Tape [audio/video]
Film
Print [unilateral]

5. Dialect

Regional

Understand British standard English dialect
Understand RP or near RP accents [variety not specifiable]
Produce West African standard English dialect, Northern Nigerian accent.

Temporal

Contemporary

6. Target level

Dimensions

	Medium			
	Spoken		Written	
	Receive	Produce	Receive	Produce
Size of utterance/text	6	3	7	3
Complexity of utterance/text	7	4	6	5
Range of forms/ micro — {functions skills	5	4	5	5
Delicacy of forms/ micro — {functions skills	5	5	6	6
Speed of communications	6	4	3/5	3/6
Flexibility of communication	3/5	2/5	3	3

Conditions

	Medium			
	Spoken		Written	
	Receive	Produce	Receive	Produce
Tolerance of:				
Error/linguistic)	3	4	3	3
Stylistic failure	4	4	5	4
Reference (to dictionary, addressee etc)	3	4	2/5	2/5
Repetition (re-read/ ask for repeat)	3	—	2/5	—
Hesitation (lack of fluency)	—	4	—	—

7. Communicative events activities

Event 1

Business studies student attending lectures in his central and optional areas of study

Activities:
Listening for overall comprehension and selective retention
Taking notes that can be re-constituted
Asking for clarification
[for subject matter, see note below Event 6]

Event 2

Business Studies student participating in seminars and tutorials in central and optional areas of study

Activities
Discussing topics from previous lectures or related topics, presented by seminar/tutorial leader
Listening for overall comprehension, taking notes and asking for clarification (as above).

Event 3

Business Studies student studying reference materials (textbooks, manuals/articles/lecture, seminar handouts/realia) in English in university library, private study

Activities
Reading intensively to understand all the information in a text
Reading for the main information in a text
Reading for specific assignment-oriented information
Reading to discover and assess writer's position on a particular issue

Event 4

Business Studies student writing notes, reports and essays in central and optional areas of study

Activities

Selecting, sorting and sequencing information for reports or essays
Writing factual accounts of theories, practices and trends
Writing evaluative reports/essays on theories, practices and procedures

Event 5

Business Studies student keeping up-to-date with current literature (new books/periodicals etc) in areas of study and related fields

Activities

Reading as a routine check on new information and its possible relevance to areas of study
Reading to assess desirability of text for intensive study
Reading extensively in search of information required from sources not given

Event 6

Business Studies student participating in official industrial and commercial visits

Activities

Discussing topics raised by personnel contacted on official industrial and commercial visits
Raising and discussing matters observed during the course of industrial and commercial visits

Subject matter for all activities

Referential vocabulary categories/topics related to the relevant areas of study ie Economics; Legal Studies; Business Accounts; Statistics; Marketing; Purchasing

8. Communicative key

For events 1, 2, 6

Receptive	*Productive*
Cautious – incautious	pleasant
Caring – indifferent	cautious
Formal – informal	caring
Courteous – discourteous	formal – informal
Disinterested – biased	courteous
Praising – detracting	patient
Approving – disapproving	grateful (acknowledging)
Willing – unwilling	honest
Inducive – dissuasive	disinterested
Active – inactive	respectful
Concordant – discordant	pleasing
Authoritative – lacking	approving – disapproving/
in authority	regretting
Compelling – uncompelling	willing
Certain – uncertain	inducive – dissuasive
Intelligent/thinking –	active
	concordant
Unthinking/unintelligent	authoritative
	compelling
Assenting – dissenting	certain – uncertain
	rational
	assenting – dissenting

For events 3, 4, 5

Receptive

Cautious – incautious
Caring – indifferent

Formal – informal
Honest – dishonest
Disinterested – biased
Approving – disapproving
Inducive – dissuasive
Concordant – discordant
Authoritative – lacking in authority
Compelling – uncompelling
Certain – uncertain
Intelligent/thinking – unthinking/unintelligent
Assenting – dissenting

9. Language/communication skills specification

Skill
number

9   Recognizing the use of stress in connected speech

   1. For indicating information units:
   content words and form words
   rhythmic patterning.

   2. For emphasis, through location of nuclear shift.
   3. For contrast, through nuclear shift.

15   Interpreting attitudinal meaning through:

   1. Pitch height
   2. Pitch range
   3. Pause
   4. Tempo.

16   Deducing the meaning and use of unfamiliar lexical items
through

   1. Understanding word formation:
   Stems/roots;
   affixation;

Skill
number

derivation;
compounding.
2. Contextual clues.

20   Understanding explicitly-stated information.

21   Expressing information explicity.

22   Understanding information in the text, not explicitly stated, through:

Making inferences.

24   Understanding conceptual meaning, especially:

1. Quantity and amount.
2. Definiteness and indefiniteness.
3. Comparison; degree.
4. Time (especially aspect).

6. Means; instrument.
7. Cause; result; purpose; reason; condition; contrast.

25   Expressing conceptual meaning, especially:

1. Quantity and amount.
2. Definiteness and indefiniteness.
3. Comparison; degree.
4. Time (especially tense and aspect).
5. Location; direction.
6. Means; instrumental
7. Cause; result; purpose; reason; condition; contrast.

26/27   Understanding and expressing the communicative value of text/utterances with and without explicit indicators in respect of the following micro-functions:

1. Scale of certainty

Certainty

Probability
Possibility
Nil certainty
Conviction
Conjecture
Doubt
Disbelief

2. Scale of commitment

Intention
Obligation

3. Judgement and evaluation

Valuation

Verdiction.
exempt, conciliate, extenuate;
approve, value, merit, entitle.

Disapproval:
disapprove, complain, allege, accuse, reprimand, condemn.

4. Suasion

Inducement:
persuade, propose, advise, recommend; advocate.

Compulsion:
order, direct, compel, oblige, prohibit, disallow.

Prediction:
predict, warn, caution;
instruct, invite.

Tolerance:
allow, grant, consent to, authorize.

Skill
number

5. Argument

Information:
State, inform, report;
declare, assert, emphasize, maintain; argue, advocate, claim.

Question; request.

Deny, disclaim, protest; oppose, refuse, reject; disprove, negate.

Agreement:
Agree, assent; endorse, ratify.

Disagreement:
Disagree, dissent; dispute, repudiate.

Concession:
Concede, grant, admit; withdraw, retract, resign.

6. Rational enquiry

Proposition; corollary.
Substantiation, proof.
Assumption.
Conclusion, generalization.
Demonstration, explanation.
Classification, definition, exemplification.

28   Understanding relations within the sentence, especially:

long premodification, and postmodification, especially postmodification by prepositional phrase.

29   Expressing relations within the sentence, especially:

Premodification, postmodification and disjuncts;

Complex embedding.

Skill
number

30   Understanding relations between parts of a text through lexical cohesion devices, especially:

Lexical set/collocation

31   Expressing relations between parts of a text through lexical cohesion devices, especially:

Synonymy

Hyponymy;

Lexical set/collocation.

32   Understanding relations between part of a text through grammatical cohesion devices, especially:

Reference
Substitution
Ellipsis
Logical connectors.

33   Expressing relations between parts of a text through grammatical cohesion devices, especially:

Reference
Substitution
Ellipsis
Time and place relaters
Logical connectors.

34   Interpreting text by going outside it:

Using exophonic reference;
'Reading between the lines';
Integrating data in the text with own experience or knowledge of the world.

*Skill
number*

35   Recognizing indicators in discourse for:

Transition to a new idea;
Anticipating an objection or contrary view

36   Using indicators in discourse for:

Developing an idea;
Transition to another idea;
Concluding an idea;
Anticipating an objection or contrary view.

37   Identifying the main point or important information in a
piece of discourse, through:

Vocal underlining;
Verbal cues;
Topic sentences, in paragraphs of inductive and deductive
organization.

38   Indicating the main point or important information in a
piece of discourse, through:

Verbal cues

39   Distinguishing the main idea from supporting details by
differentiating:

The whole from its parts;
Fact from opinion;
A proposition from its argument.

40   Extracting salient points to summarize:

The whole text;
A specific idea/topic in the text;
The underlying ideas or point of the text.

41   Selective extraction of relevant points from a text, involving:

The co-ordination of related information;

*Skill
number*

The ordered rearrangement of contrasting items;
The tabulation of information for comparison and contrast.

42   Expanding salient/relevant points into a summary of:

The whole text;
A specific idea/topic in the text.

43   Reducing the text through rejecting redundant or irrelevant information and items, especially:

Use of abbreviations;
Use of symbols.

44   Basic reference skills: understanding and use of:

Graphic presentation, *viz* headings, sub-headings, numbering;
Cross-referencing;
Card catalogue.

45   Skimming to obtain:

The gist of the text;
A general impression of the text.

46   Scanning to locate specifically required information on:

A single point, involving a complex search;
More than one point, involving a complex search;
A whole topic.

47   Initiating in discourse:

How to initiate the discourse.

48   Maintaining the discourse:

How to respond;
How to continue;
How to adapt as a result of feedback;

How to turn take;
How to mark time.

49   Terminating in discourse:

How to come out of the discourse.

50   Planning and organizing information in expository language (especially presentation of reports, expounding an argument, evaluation of evidence, using rhetorical functions, such as those specified in 26 above.

51   Transcoding information presented in diagrammatic display, involving:

Conversion of diagram/table/graph into speech/writing;
Interpretation or comparison of diagrams/tables/graphs in speech/writing.

52   Transcoding information in speech/writing to diagrammatic display, through:

Completing a diagram/table/graph;
Constructing one or more diagrams/tables/graphs.

Appendix II. Information banks for test development

Excerpts from a communicative test specification prepared for the Royal Society of Arts

(Brendan J Carroll, July 1978, adapted from the original specification by Shelagh Rixon)

Note:

The order of the information banks in this specification is slightly different from that outlined in Figure 5 (p. 24 above).

Bank 1: Level

(broad categories in a progress continuum)

Basic;
Intermediate;
Advanced.

Bank 2: Mode

(focuses rather than exclusive macro-activities)

Listening;
Speaking;
Reading;
Writing;
Integrated (L+S+R+W).

Bank 3: Performance criterion

Size;   Accuracy;
Complexity;   Appropriacy;
Range;   Independence;
Speed;   Repetition;
Flexibility;   Hesitation.

The first five criteria are available mainly for test writing, the second five mainly but not exclusively for performance assessment. See Appendix I for detailed specification of criteria.

Bank 4: Event

Taking part in social interaction;
Visiting places of interest;
Shopping and using services;
Travel in Britain and elsewhere;
Obtaining medical attention and health services;
Eating and drinking in public places;
Using media for entertainment and information;
Studying for interest and information;
Reading for pleasure;
Conducting personal correspondence;
Dealing with officials.

Bank 5: Activity

Activities are arranged roughly in ascending order of potential difficulty.

1. Social

Conduct polite or phatic conversation;
Discuss one's own language performance;
Give details of personal background;
Ask for clarification of information;
Discuss current events, weather, sport;
Handle instructions, thanks, complaints;
Discuss life in Britain and elsewhere;
Conduct mealtime conversation;
Understand operating instructions (eg use of radio);
Give opinions on general subjects.

2. Places of interest

Understand descriptions by guide/friend;
Ask for clarification of information;
Ask for directions to a location;
Read notes and handouts;
Book and buy tickets for visit;
Read books, brochures on place;
Search for further information;
Give appreciative or critical comment.

3. Shopping

Gain attention on arrival;
Discuss services or goods required;
Give decision on purchase;
Pay or discuss method of payment;
Understand money system;
Make spoken or written complaints;
Make orders by telephone;
Examine forms re purchase;
Complete guarantee, hire purchase forms.

4. Travel

State destination and request fare;
Ask for directions;
Understand road signs and symbols;
Study timetables and schedules;
Read instructions, maps, and diagrams;
Understand spoken descriptions of maps/diagrams;
Negotiate customs and visa formalities;
Arrange accommodation in hotel or lodgings.

5. Medical

Make appointments in person, by letter, by phone;
Give symptoms and respond to questions;
Understand directions for treatment;
Read medical forms and documents;
Complete forms and declarations;
Make written and spoken queries re treatment.

6. Meals, drinks

Gain attention on arrival;
Ask for menu, place orders;
Request bill and make payment;
Arrange booking by phone;
Modify orders, appreciate, complain.

7. Media

Read TV and radio schedules and announcements;
Discuss radio, TV, recorder controls;
Take calls and make enquiries by phone;
Understand radio, TV news announcements;
Discuss TV, radio current affairs and drama;
Read media periodicals and critiques;
Follow film, play, TV series, documentaries.

8. Studying

Participate in a language lesson;
Use simplified dictionary;
Use basic reference books;
Understand talks and debates, make queries;
Obtain and share views in seminars;
Take and write up from notes;
Use library for reference and instruction;
Discuss one's occupational experiences and interests;
Write reports, essays and examination answers;
Research files for information, present summaries.

9. Reading

Read news headlines and simple reports;
Read contents and synopsis pages of magazines;
Discuss headlines and illustrations;
Read magazine articles, news reports, editorials, correspondence, short stories;
Read full novels and poems;
Group discussion of impressions of above writing.

10. Correspondence

Write short notes;
Write personal letters;
Write diary and personal reports of events.

11. Officials

Read forms and instructions;
Complete forms requiring basic information;
Discuss needs with officials;
Reply to official letters;
Complete complex forms and questionaires;
Continue correspondence to pursue one's case;
Argue case face-to-face with official.

Bank 6: Topic area

— related to events as listed above —

1. Social

Polite conversation, greetings, weather, food, drink, games and athletics, family relationships, professions, jobs, money, furniture, utensils, language descriptive terms.

2. Places of interest

Building and architectural terms, geography, dates, history, location, direction, parts and towns of Britain, money, transport.

3. Shopping

Parts of shop, sales staff, departments, clothing, food, drink, cosmetics, books, papers, electrical goods.

4. Travel

Fares, tickets, maps, schedules, vehicles, traffic, terminals, stations, airports, customs, passports, visas, types of accommodation, terms and conditions of rental.

5. Medical

Types of medical practice, health service, illness, symptoms, parts of body, medical documents, medicines, types of treatment, parts of hospital, medical staff.

6. Meals, drinks

Food, drink, cooking, menus, seating, tableware, diets, bills.

7. Media

Types of programme, media personalities, film stars, sports celebrities, government, economics, international relations, media hardware, and software, telephone use, musicians.

8. Studying

Language schools and classes, language terms, novels, reference books, poems, common occupations, examination instructions.

9. Reading

Editorials, news items, weeklies, serious periodicals, advertising sections, higher reading, illustrations, criticism.

10. Correspondence

Writing conventions, everyday events, social functions.

11. Officials

Documents, visas, licences, regulations, currency, financial and domestic circumstances, consulates, customs, police, rent, grants, work permits.

Bank 7: Notions/functions

1. Social

(Note: greetings will be needed in most interpersonal contexts) greet, introduce, fare-well, apologize, invite, accept, enquire, inform, thank, open, acknowledge, agree, disagree, persuade,

2. Visiting

Assess, judge, approve, suggest, advise, inform, invite, decline, explain, query.

3. Shopping

Query, prefer, assure, judge, excuse, complain, deplore, suggest, urge, claim, deny, dissent, explain, illustrate, agree, conviction, certainty, doubt, negation.

4. Travel

Believe, anticipate, assume, intend, prefer, oblige, estimate, excuse, appreciate, suggest, agree, claim, request, explain, probability, possibility.

5. Medical

Estimate, undertake, choice, complain, query, deduce, agree, comply, emphasize, consent, conclude, illustrate, explain, possibility, negation, frequency, duration, intensity, conviction, doubt.

6. Eating

Order, emphasize, estimate, compare, negate, choose, complain, enquire, agree, illustrate, acknowledge, confirm, explain.

7. Media

Assess, judge, commend, appreciate, disapprove, agree, disagree, clarify, illustrate.

8. Studying

Inform, interpret, verify, prove, deduce, generalize, explain, define, confirm, query, certainty, probability, negation, conviction, supposition.

9. Reading

Emphasize, affirm, argue, advocate, approve, concede; *valuation* – assessment, judging, verdiction, pronounce, find; *argu-*

ment – report, emphasize, affirm, argue, advocate; *agreement* – concur, confirm, support; *disagreement* – dissent, dispute, contradict.

10. Correspondence

Introductory, formulae (written), greeting, farewell, thanks, apology, congratulations, statement, report, emphasize.

11. Officials

Persuade, beg, urge, suggest, maintain, protest, repute, deny, concede, allow, defer, submit, certainty, negation, conviction, doubt.

Bank 8: Attitudinal tones

The attitudinal tone index derives from the social relationships of the participants with their interlocuters. All tones should be recognized by the participants in due course, but not all need to be produced by them, eg 'unpleasant'. Further subdivisions of the categories may be used (taken from the Munby bank) as necessary.
eg 'formal – informal' (stiff, chatty, etc)
Approving – disapproving;
Assenting – dissenting;
Authoritative – unauthoritative;
Caring – indifferent;
Cautious – incautious;
Certain – uncertain;
Courteous – discourteous;
Entertaining – tedious;
Formal – informal;
Friendly – unfriendly;
Grateful – ungrateful;
Honest – dishonest;
Humorous – humourless;
Inducive – dissuasive;

Intelligent – unintelligent;
Pleasant – unpleasant;
Praising – derogatory;
Regretting – unregretting;
Respectful – disrespectful;
Sociable – unsociable.

Bank 9: Language skills

Please refer to Language/communication skills specification in Appendix I above (p. 115 ff), and select appropriate skills.

Bank 10: Miscellaneous aspects

1. Channels

Face-to-face (dialogue and monologue), print, tape, public address, radio, telephone, disc, TV, film.

2. Social relationships

Outsider – insider;
English speaker – non-English speaker;
Woman to man;
Woman to woman;
Man to man;
Learner – instructor;
Guest – host;
Adult – adult;
Employee – employer;
Stranger – stranger;
Member of public – employee.

3. Dialect

The participant should be able eventually to understand Standard English with the national varieties of Scottish, Welsh and Irish and local varieties such as London, West Country, Lancashire, Yorkshire and Midlands (none of the above in 'extreme' versions).

They should be able to produce a version of Standard English which, although influenced by their mother-tongue features, can be understood without difficulty or strain by an educated native-user.

Reprinted by kind permission of the Royal Society of Arts Examinations Board.
N.B. The Board wish to make it clear that the data banks reproduced here were commissioned at an early stage of the design of a new series of examinations. They should not be taken as representing the final basis on which their examinations have been constructed.

Appendix III. Sample rating scales

1. General assessment scale

Band

9	**Expert user.** Communicates with authority, accuracy and style. Completely at home in idiomatic and specialist English.
8	**Very good user.** Presentation of subject clear and logical with fair style and appreciation of attitudinal markers. Often approaching bi-lingual competence.
7	**Good user.** Would cope in most situations in an English-speaking environment. Occasional slips and restrictions of language will not impede communication.
6	**Competent user.** Although coping well with most situations he is likely to meet, is somewhat deficient in fluency and accuracy and will have occasional misunderstandings or significant errors.
5	**Modest user.** Although he manages in general to communicate, often uses inaccurate or inappropriate language.
4	**Marginal user.** Lacking in style, fluency and accuracy, is not easy to communicate with, accent and usage cause misunderstandings. Generally can get by without serious breakdowns.
3	**Extremely limited user.** Does not have a working knowledge of the language for day-to-day purposes, but better than an absolute beginner. Neither productive or receptive skills allow continuous communication.
2	**Intermittent user.** Performance well below level of a working day-to-day knowledge of the language. Communication occurs only sporadically.
1/0	**Non-user.** May not even recognize with certainty which language is being used.

2. Interview assessment scale

Band

9	**Expert speaker.** Speaks with authority on a variety of topics. Can initiate, expand and develop a theme.
8	**Very good non-native speaker.** Maintains effectively his own part of a discussion. Initiates, maintains and elaborates as necessary. Reveals humour where needed and responds to attitudinal tones.
7	**Good speaker.** Presents case clearly and logically and can develop the dialogue coherently and constructively. Rather less flexible and fluent than Band 8 performer but can respond to main changes of tone or topic. Some hesitation and repetition due to a measure of language restriction but interacts effectively.
6	**Competent speaker.** Is able to maintain theme of dialogue, to follow topic switches and to use and appreciate main attitude markers. Stumbles and hesitates at times but is reasonably fluent otherwise. Some errors and inappropriate language but these will not impede exchange of views. Shows some independence in discussion with ability to initiate.
5	**Modest speaker.** Although gist of dialogue is relevant and can be basically understood, there are noticeable deficiencies in mastery of language patterns and style. Needs to ask for repetition or clarification and similarly to be asked for them. Lacks flexibility and initiative. The interviewer often has to speak rather deliberately. Copes but not with great style or interest.
4	**Marginal speaker.** Can maintain dialogue but in a rather passive manner, rarely taking initiative or guiding the discussion. Has difficulty in following English at normal speed; lacks fluency and probably accuracy in speaking. The dialogue is therefore neither easy nor flowing. Nevertheless, gives the impression that he is in touch with the gist of the dialogue even if not wholly master of it. Marked L1 accent.
3	**Extremely limited speaker.** Dialogue is a drawn-out affair punctuated with hesitations and misunderstandings. Only catches part of normal speech and unable to produce continuous and accurate discourse. Basic merit is just hanging on to discussion gist, without making major contribution to it.
2	**Intermittent speaker.** No working facility; occasional, sporadic communication.
1/0	**Non-speaker.** Not able to understand and/or speak.

3. Academic writing scale

Band

9	**Expert writer.** Writes with authority, accuracy and style. Has a mastery of appropriate and concise English.
8	**Very good writer.** Clear and logical presentation with accurate language forms and good style. Just the occasional slip or infelicity reveals he is not a native writer. Often approaching bi-lingual competence.
7	**Good writer.** Can develop a thesis systematically with well-structured main and subordinate themes and relevant supporting detail. Generally accurate and appropriate language, layout and style. Responds to tone or purpose of writing task. Mainly distinguished from Band 8 performer in fluency, accuracy and appropriateness.
6	**Competent writer.** Uses a wide range of skills to convey thesis – presenting it in quite a well-structured fashion, arranging main and supporting themes and details logically. Use of lexis and grammatical patterns reasonably accurate. Slight limitation of style and mastery of appropriate idiom in an otherwise intelligible presentation.
5	**Modest writer.** Conveys basic information competently, but logical structure of presentation will lack clarity. Work will show several slips and formal errors. Use of style and conveyance of tone is present but not consistent. Essay may well lack interest but the basic message gets through.
4	**Marginal writer.** Presentation has coherent appearance and several factual statements can be sequentially made. Work lacks logical structure and use of discourse markers. Often makes lexical and grammatical errors. Uses basic punctuation conventions. Uses restricted range of skills. Will backtrack and may still repeat. Basic theme is conveyed but imperfectly.
3	**Extremely limited writer.** Produces a string of sentences rather than an essay. Some theme but not logically presented. Use of simple sentence structure and restricted lexis with errors and inappropriacies abounding. Main merit is the conveyance of straightforward information.
2	**Intermittent writer.** No working facility: perhaps sporadic uses.
1/0	**Non-writer.** Not able to write.

4. Oral interaction assessment scale

Advanced Level (equivalent to Band 7.0, 'L' score 70 or above)

Size	Can understand and take part effectively in an extended dialogue or group discussion.
Complexity	Can handle several major topics with their subsidiary points, coping with noise and irregularities in flow of dialogue.
Range	Can describe and explain events, graphics and objects/equipment using a wide range of skills, functions and tones.
Speed	Copes with speech at normal speed, responds promptly speaking neither too slowly nor hesitantly.
Flexibility	Maintains comprehension when listening to varied speeds of delivery, different voices and accents and switches of emphasis in topic. Can change topic if appropriate. Handles interjections and interpolations well.
Accuracy	Interprets accurately lexical and grammatical usage and intonation and stress patterns, also appreciates communicative value of an utterance. Use of grammar, lexis, intonation and stress effective although likely to have some non-English features.
Appropriacy	Understands and uses contemporary English with a variety (eg slang and idiom) suitable to the particular setting and social relationship involved.
Independence	Rarely has to query speaker for clarification.
Repetition	Does not often have to ask for repetition of statement.
Hesitation	Has no prolonged hesitations or false starts, to an extent more than a native speaker.
Overall	*Is a responsive and effective conversationalist, able to handle with social adequacy the specified events and activities. Comprehends well and speaks fluently; would have no difficulty in surviving in an English-speaking environment.*

5. Oral interaction assessment scale

Intermediate Level (equivalent to Band 5.5 or 'L' score of 55 minimum)

Size	Can participate in a discussion with several people keeping in touch with the gist even if occasional lack of grasp of details.
Complexity	Can understand and discuss one or two major points and supporting details. Can make a firm point but disturbed by noise and distractions.
Range	Can describe and discuss implications of events, graphics and objects using a number of language skills and tones.
Speed	Will have breaks in comprehension in normal, rapid speech presentations and his own speech will be of less than native tempo for stretches.
Flexibility	Can cope with occasional but not frequent switches of topic and style of presentation. Recognizes when a different type of utterance, such as a joke, is being used, and changes his own style accordingly.
Accuracy	Does not seriously misinterpret overt meaning of utterance but not quite so ready to understand implied meaning. Uses language at his disposal accurately and aware of his usage limitations. Accent and sometimes usage is likely to be patently foreign.
Appropriacy	Appreciates major styles of presentation including some slang and regional usages, but can be puzzled by such deviations from the norm. Does not always use slang appropriately or adapt style of presentation.
Independence	Will not often have to ask for clarification unless presentation is unusually rapid or confusing. Can 'speak on his feet' but needs more recourse to preparation and notes than would a fully competent speaker.
Repetition	May ask for repetition if speech is rapid or extended.
Hesitation	Prone to more false starts and space-fillers than a fully competent speaker.
Overall	*A useful participant in a discussion or interview. Keeps in touch with main points and able to put over his own point of view but level of comprehension and fluency lies between Basic and Advanced level performances.*

6. Oral Interaction assessment scale

Basic Level (equivalent to Band 4.0 or 'L' score 40 minimum)

Size	Understands an utterance of 2 or 3 sentences, or extracts from a longer text 2 or 3 specified items of information. Gets the gist of a simple short conversation and obeys simple instructions. Can make an appropriate statement, description or response of 2 or 3 sentences.
Complexity	Understands a main point with one or two subsidiary details. Can make a short description of an event and an object present or absent. Easily confused by noise.
Range	Understands and uses a relevant if restricted range of skills and tones related to common social activities such as travel, basic greetings, family relationships and simple commercial activities.
Speed	Although not needing unnaturally slow enunciation, sometimes has to be addressed somewhat deliberately. Speaks with some unevenness of tempo.
Flexibility	Finds it difficult to adjust to changes of topic, tempo and voice. Does not adjust readily in response to his listener's reactions.
Accuracy	Appreciates and expresses the significant elements of an utterance, using correctly the basic intonation, stress, lexical and grammatical patterns. Reasonably accurate within his repertoire.
Appropriacy	Not responsive to stylistic and tone nuances and does not readily adopt style to occasion. May misuse idioms.
Independence	Needs to ask for clarification from interlocutor and may require occasional assistance whilst speaking.
Repetition	Will have to ask for repetition or else miss significance of extended, rapid discourse. Often over-uses stock formulae.
Hesitation	Will fairly often have to search for words or hold his place with 'ums' and 'ers'.
Overall	*Partial comprehension with limited fluency in conversing, but able to manage and survive in an English-speaking society if some tolerance is extended to him.*

Appendix IV. Correlation matrices

1. Three correlation matrices for (a) initial (b) mid and (c) final testing in English of 156 Spanish speaking students. (Decimal points omitted.)

Variable		1 Com-preh	2 Essay	3 Cloze (ac)	4 Cloze (ex)	5 Struct	6 Dict	7 Sp(ac)	8 Sp(ex)
1. Compre-hension	a		408	602	551	444	431	383	447
	b		411	363	413	405	352	195	097
	c		355	461	431	472	422	424	430
2. Essay	a	408		541	511	452	498	308	351
	b	411		545	563	523	457	431	318
	c	355		529	480	430	584	270	302
3. Cloze (acc)	a	602	541		963	534	536	388	436
	b	363	545		929	469	558	304	172
	c	461	529		899	623	621	468	447
4. Cloze (exact)	a	551	511	963		543	504	361	398
	b	413	563	929		484	562	311	211
	c	431	480	899		587	614	455	423
5. Structure	a	444	452	534	543		466	308	293
	b	405	523	469	484		554	220	102
	c	472	430	623	587		590	468	486
6. Dictation	a	431	498	536	504	466		330	380
	b	352	457	558	562	554		314	231
	c	422	584	621	614	590		421	426
7. Spanish (acc)	a	383	308	388	361	308	330		859
	b	195	431	304	311	220	314		813
	c	424	270	468	455	468	421		931
8. Spanish (ex)	a	447	351	436	398	293	380	859	
	b	097	318	172	211	102	231	813	
	c	430	302	447	423	486	426	931	
9. Class grade	a	408	456	559	494	411	497	416	425
	b	191	330	313	302	354	427	305	178
	c	365	415	358	360	315	464	368	417

2. Principal component analyses of the three correlation matrices above

Components for matrix (a)	1 Compreh	2 Essay	3 Cl (ac)	4 Cl (ex)	5 Struct	6 Dict	7 Sp (ac)	8 Sp (ex)
%55.9 i	384	310	356	268	273	621	221	224
13.9 ii	447	019	215	163	069	−729	325	290
10.1 iii	225	178	292	247	234	−187	−624	−542
7.6 iv	686	−601	−159	−158	−221	209	−139	−078
Matrix (b)	1	2	3	4	5	6	7	8
%54.4 i	267	351	276	244	441	668	179	101
12.3 ii	397	436	092	103	128	−663	348	237
11.6 iii	356	−062	−013	−004	504	−209	−578	−487
8.3 iv	714	−130	095	100	−641	165	−101	−079
matrix (c)	1	2	3	4	5	6	7	8
%58.0 i	252	296	414	278	424	474	326	302
14.1 ii	082	−340	−183	−123	−047	−348	622	565
7.9 iii	163	−449	332	216	560	−482	−180	−191
6.8 iv	153	−146	−589	−400	579	325	−100	−028

Notes: The sum of square equals unity for each component.
Decimal points omitted.

Bibliography

Alexander, L G (1977) *Waystage and threshold level: Some methodological implications* Council of Europe, Strasbourg.*

Brière, E J (1968) Current trends in language testing *TESOL Quarterly* 3,4, 333–340.
Brière, E J (1971) Are we really measuring proficiency with our foreign language tests? *Foreign Language Annals*, vol 4, May.

Candlin, C N (1976) 'Communicative language teaching and the debt to pragmatics' in Ramch, C (ed) *Semantics: theory and application* Georgetown University Press.
Candlin, C N, C J Bruton and **J H Leather** (1974) *English language skills for overseas doctors and medical staff* Reports 1 – 4 and Appendices 1 – 2, Linguistics Section, Department of English, University of Lancaster.
Candlin, C N, C J Bruton, J H Leather and **G Woods** (1976) *Doctor-patient communication skills* Medical Recording Service Foundation, Chelmsford.
Candlin, C N, J M Kirkwood, and **H M Moore** (1975) 'Developing study skills in English' in *English for academic study* British Council, English Teaching Information Centre.
Candlin, C N, J H Leather and **C J Bruton** (1976) Doctors in casualty *IRAL*, 14, 3.
Carroll, B J (1978) *Specifications for an English Language Testing Service,* British Council, London.
Clark, J L D (1972) *Foreign language testing: theory and practice* Center for Curriculum Development, Philadelphia, PA.
Council of Europe see *A European unit/credit system for Modern Language learning by adults* Strasbourg (1978).

van Ek, J A 'The threshold level in a unit/credit system' in *Systems development in adult language learning* Council of Europe, Strasbourg.*

Ervin–Tripp, S (1964) 'An analysis of the interaction of language topic and listener' in Argyle, M (ed) *Social encounters* Penguin edn (1973).
Ervin–Tripp, S (1972) 'On socio-linguistic rules: alternation and co-occurrence' in Gumperz and Hymes (eds) *Directions in socio-linguistics* Holt–Rinehart.

Fishman, J A (1978) 'The sociolinguistic foundation of language testing' in Spolsky, B *Papers in Applied Linguistics,* Center for Applied Linguistics, Arlington, Virginia.

Foreign Service Institute (1978) 'Development and use of the FSI oral interview test' (H E Sollenberger) in Clark, J L D (*ed*) *Direct testing of speaking proficiency* Educational Testing Service, Princeton, NJ.

Hymes, D (1974) 'Towards ethnographies of communication: the analysis of communicative events' in Giglioli (*ed*) *Language and social context* Penguin.

Jakobovits, L A, (1970) *Foreign language learning,* Newbury House, Rowley, Mass. and (1968) *see* references p. 323 of above work.

Morrow, K E (1977) *Techniques of evaluation for a notional syllabus* Royal Society of Arts.

Morrow, K E (1978) 'Communicative language testing: revolution or evolution?' in Brumfit, C J and K Johnson (*eds*) *The Communicative approach to language teaching* Oxford University Press.

Munby, J L (1978) *Communicative syllabus design* Cambridge University Press.

Popham, W J, and **T R Husek** (1969) Implications of criterion-referenced measurement *Journal of Educational Measurement*, 6, 1.

Rea, P M (1978) Assessing language as communication *MALS Journal* University of Birmingham.

Roos–Wijgh, I F (1978) 'Testing speaking proficiency through functional dialogues', Dutch National Institute for Educational Measurement, in Clark (*ed*) *Direct testing of speaking proficiency*, ETS, Princeton.

Sinclair, J McH, I J Forsyth, R M Coulthard and **H Ashby** (1972) *The English used by teachers and pupils: final report to the SSRC* University of Birmingham.

Spolsky, B, P Murphy, W Holm and **A Ferrel** (1972) Functional tests of oral fluency *TESOL Quarterly*, Sept.

Stevenson, D K (1979) *Beyond faith and face validity* Unpublished paper for TESOL Convention, Boston.

Trim, J L M (1973) 'Draft outline of a European unit/credit system' in *Systems development in adult language learning* Council of Europe, Strasbourg.*

Upshur, J A *Measurement of oral communication* Undated mimeo, University of Michigan.

Widdowson, H G (1975) 'EST in theory and practice' in *English for academic study* British Council, English Teaching Information Centre.

Widdowson, H G (1978) *Teaching language as communication* Oxford University Press, Oxford.

Widdowson, H G (1979) *Explorations in applied linguistics* Oxford University Press, Oxford.

Wilkins, D A (1978) 'The general structure of a unit/credit system for adult language learning' in Trim, J L M *Some possible lines of development of an overall structure for a European unit/credit scheme* Council of Europe, Strasbourg.*

*The Council of Europe Modern Language Project Series is now published by Pergamon Press Ltd, Headington Hill Hall, Oxford.

Acknowledgement

Permission to include an extract on 'Demand and supply' from *A textbook of economic theory* (1972) by A W Stonier and D C Hague was given by the Longman Group Ltd, Longman House, Burnt Mill, Harlow, Essex, and by John Wiley Inc, 605 Third Avenue, NY 10016.

Index